BULL$#✻! ARTIST

❖ ❖ ❖

THE 9/11 LEADERSHIP MYTH

Ron Schalow

BULL$#*! ARTIST

THE 9/11 LEADERSHIP MYTH

To ORDER ADDITIONAL COPIES, PLEASE CONTACT US.

BOOKSURGE, LLC

WWW.BOOKSURGE.COM

1-866-308-6235

ORDERS@BOOKSURGE.COM

PRINTED IN THE UNITED STATES OF AMERICA

COVER AND INTERIOR DESIGN BY
REZAC DESIGN STUDIO AND REBECCA KNUTSON, FARGO, ND

COVER PHOTO BY GETTY IMAGES

FOR MY PARENTS

CONTENTS

Introduction

"Conservatives saw the savagery of 9/11 and the attacks
and prepared for war; liberals saw the savagery of the 9/11 attacks
and wanted to prepare indictments and offer therapy
and understanding for our attackers."
—KARL ROVE JUNE 6, 2005

Summer 2005: Osama is still on the loose. The number of terrorist attacks worldwide has risen exponentially. Afghanistan is a mess. Oceans of blood have been spilled to see a dictator in his underwear. Billions of dollars, and thousands of lives and limbs, have been spent to establish many parts of Iraq as terrorist havens. The United States is heavily in debt, more Americans are poor, torture is an accepted government policy and blowing the cover of U.S. spies is no longer a big deal. George Bush is presiding over a Ponzi scheme where wealth pours in at the bottom of the pyramid and the president passes it out at the pointy end. Everything is just swell.

Nevertheless—a majority of Americans continue to give the small man the benefit of the doubt. More than half still believe Bush to be a rough and tumble leader who led the nation on 9/11—the great guardian, tough on terror and the best hope to ward off the evildoers. Some say the president is so masculine that when he clears brush on his manly Texas ranch, hair grows on the dead branches he casts aside—even when he wears gloves— thick leather gloves. The legendary 9/11 leadership storyline still thrills the segregated crowds and George Bush and his minions are always primed to flash the dog-eared 9/11 card—it's the only one they have left in the deck.

Those not on board with GW, the ones not allowed at the president's appearances, are labeled as irrational Bush haters, un-American and traitors. The politically correct police are sent out to hammer anyone with the audacity to offend the tender sensibilities of the president. If Bush lies, it's unacceptable to say Bush lied. He misstated, misremembered or was factually distant from the truth—but he didn't lie. It's downright rude to call the straight shooting liar a liar.

Then in September 2005, while humans drowned, starved, dehydrated and died on American soil, the Texas Tortoise opted to continue with his umpteenth vacation and make a few photo-op appearances in several states to the west of Louisiana with lower humidity and lighter breezes. Finally, after days of Katrina carnage, White House staffers drew straws to determine which poor sap would have to tell the petty prince that he had to go back to work—or at least roll up his shirt sleeves for the cameras.

At last, even people not prone to paying attention realized that Bush 43 is incredibly incompetent. And—as if his indifference to the current crisis weren't enough, we also learned that the President of the United States cared so little about the safety of the American people that he stocked agencies responsible for our protection with unskilled friends and supporters—an incompetent hiring incompetents…cronyism, nepotism, incest and affirmative action at the highest level. The grand defender is a gigantic phony.

It shouldn't have been a shocker. George Bush blew the big one before—he responded to the attacks on 9/11 with the same ineptitude—a not so subtle indicator of things to come. Unfortunately, the president's clueless, weak-kneed and cowardly performance on that day passed by largely without scrutiny and most Americans didn't get the full story. Normally, the President of the United States can't trim his toenails without news coverage and days of analysis, but somehow—on one of the most historically significant days in the life of this nation, several hours of the Commander-in-Chief's day have gone missing—simply kicked under the bleachers—historical trash.

When George W. Bush saw the savagery on that day in 2001, he did absolutely nothing—no defense, no offense…zero. Faced with an unscripted situation and unversed in the basics of his job, the president frittered away the hours and then scampered off to an underground hideout below the prairie chickens—Karl Rove, the magnificent author and orator of warrior words, cowered at his side, much in need of therapy.

So, Katrina was not the first time this president was clueless and ineffectual during a life threatening crisis on American territory. The evidence proving that George Bush would be useless in an emergency was four years old by the time the people of New Orleans got a deadly taste of Bush style leadership.

On 9/11, the United States was under attack for over 100 minutes—and for over 100 minutes, the only life the Commander-in-Chief thought of saving was his own. Were he a real military man, the charge would have been dereliction of duty and failure to engage the enemy—but for the make-believe soldier, it was merely a public relations problem.

As al Qaeda terrorists seized passenger airliners and U.S. fighter jets scrambled, the president was blissfully unaware, so isolated from the actual workings of the government, he couldn't even manage to learn about the crisis taking place in the skies over his own country. Each of the four hijacked aircraft hit a target or crashed before the most powerful man in the world even knew the plane was a threat.

The CEO President was out of the loop, uninformed, unprepared and mentally deficient for the task. After repeated warnings of potential hijackings and terrorist attacks, George Bush was still surprised—like an infant playing peek-a-boo.

With the system "blinking red" the Commander-in-Chief sensed nothing suspicious when a commercial airliner crashed into the first tower of the World Trade Center and he went on with his regularly scheduled photo-op.

After the second tower was hit, Bush could not detect the subtle trend and concluded the attacks were over.

Thirty-five minutes later, the Pentagon was struck…and still the commander kept American power holstered.

Finally, 90 minutes after the first attack and 15 minutes after the fourth plane spun into the Pennsylvania countryside—when the action was totally late and completely useless, Dick Cheney instructed the president to order the Air Force to shoot down any more suicide planes. But, because of his total dependence on the vice president, Bush bypassed the chain of command and the order didn't even get through to the pilots. George Bush did one thing remotely close to leadership on that day and he bungled it.

President Bush's moment of truth had come and gone. When it came time to perform, tough talk and a manly swagger proved not to be enough. The perception of competence wouldn't save a single soul—we needed the real thing. The United States can double the half trillion dollars we spend for defense each year, but if the person at the top is weak and ignorant, it's futile. Terrorists typically don't wait patiently for slow-witted leaders to catch up.

The president didn't just dither away the seven minutes he sat stunned in the elementary school classroom—the scene made famous by Michael Moore's Fahrenheit 9/11—he squandered them all.

Luckily for this country and especially the people in Washington, D.C., passengers onboard Flight 93 did know what to do. Hostages at 30,000 feet with only cell phones and their wits, the women and men were able to figure out the plot and acted. Unlike the damp-palmed president who dallied as the attacks took place, the people on Flight 93 did something. Without daily intelligence briefs or the U.S. military at their disposal, they saved hundreds or thousands of lives. People saved by the so-called 9/11 leader—zero. All he had to show for the day was a diaper bag full of excuses.

But complete failure and the loss of 3,000 lives wasn't going to ruin George W. Bush's self esteem or compel him to do the right thing for the country by resigning in shame and sparing the nation further casualties and devastation under his watchful eye. George observed the savage murders and saw political opportunity—and he's darn proud of that day.

Bush wasn't able to bullshit his way through the terrorist attacks using his keen self-proclaimed leadership instincts, but that slight failing wasn't going to stop him from bullshitting his way out of taking responsibility for his disgraceful performance.

George Bush parlayed American death and destruction on his watch into a political trump card—that takes a real talent for shoveling the bullshit. He put lipstick on a Rove and turned his version of failed 9/11

"At any rate, I knew I had a job to do [on 9/11]. And I was quoted in the press the other day as saying I haven't regretted one thing I've decided. And that's the truth. Every decision I made, I stand by. And I'm proud of the decisions I've made."

—GEORGE BUSH DECEMBER 4, 2001

presidential leadership into the cornerstone of his administration—then turned loose the Bush-style "running of the bulls" to trample those who dared stand in his path.

Bush convinced people that he was their great protector and al Qaeda's worst enemy—despite proof of the exact opposite smoldering in New York and D.C. It was the con that opened the door for the Bush bungling to come. Without the political capital built up on the phony 9/11 premise, its unlikely George Bush would have been able to pull off his most deadly gaffe—Iraq or even be around to ignore Katrina. Arrogance and incompetence is a dangerous combination—and thousands of innocents and soldiers have paid the price.

Within hours of the attacks, the Bush administration started a marketing campaign to sell the inept and lazy president as a bold, courageous and wise leader. By mid afternoon on 9/11, advisor Karen Hughes had already lied to the nation on national television by crediting her boss for actions he never took. Then, in the evening, after the president tiptoed back to Washington, D.C., he looked directly into the camera and lied to the American people—taking credit for deeds he did not perform.

In spite of the dead and tons of rubble as evidence of his failure, the Bush team launched a campaign to sell the public on the reverse of what actually transpired—the president didn't protect the country—but that's not really important—he's still the best person to defend this country.

Sometimes coordinated, sometimes not, crudely and boldly, Bush and his accomplices bent reality, defied logic and lied—a lot. Unaccustomed to nuance or subtlety, and not bound by shame, the Bush administration remodeled the image of the air Passenger-in-Chief trembling in a Nebraska bunker into a great leader.

By the time the Republican Convention convened nearly three years later, the Bush team had transmogrified the horrific failure of 9/11 into a message of courage, foresight and testosterone. Undaunted by Bush's depiction of a cowardly stoner on 9/11, well dressed speakers Texas two-stepped to the podium to pay tribute to the little man. Many said that 9/11 went to the core of Bush's first term, and then failed to speak of any acts he in fact performed on the day. Evidently, the death of 3,000 people was only the device which triggered the dormant skills of the Midland debutante, an opening act to revealing his true leadership genius and visionary brilliance.

They took a pile of Rove and called it angel food cake.

Of course, many people with powerful voices in our government are well aware of the president's shortcomings on 9/11. Public servants of both parties looked the other way and chose to ignore the obvious, putting political, ideological or personal interests above their country. Some decided to gamble that an empty $2000 suit could keep us safe. Others opted to stay low, pray the vice president wouldn't question their patriotism and posture for the next election.

And few in the mainstream media business had the stomach for telling the truth about the Commander-in-Chief on that day. After all, there was much to report in those first days after the attacks—why let a little thing like incompetence in the Oval Office ruin the patriotic fervor and the anticipation of revenge. Many of the same journalists who covered for George Bush's 9/11 failure stood in front of the camera in 2005 with a decimated New Orleans in the background and asked, "why did it take so long for President Bush to respond?" They know why.

By the time Friday the 14th came and Bush found his so-called voice with a bullhorn on the back of an old pickup, with his arm draped pretentiously around the shoulders of an older, more experienced man who deserved to be shown some respect, instead of a pat on the head, there was no looking back. With a 90 percent approval rating gained as the direct result of his ineptitude, few would have the stones to question the imperial ruler.

This book is divided into two parts. Part one chronicles the timeline of the 9/11 terrorist attacks and the words Bush and his cronies use to discount his inaction at each juncture.

Part two details the talking points employed by the administration to lull the hand-picked crowds and adoring interviewers into the fantasy land of competent 9/11 leadership.

Most of the statements made by George Bush and apologists were

> "I think people need to be responsible for the actions they take in life. I think that—well, I think that's part of the need for a cultural change. We need to say we each need to be responsible for what we do. People in the highest office in the land must be responsible for decisions they make in life."
>
> –GEORGE BUSH
> 2000 PRESIDENTIAL DEBATES

gleaned from speeches, press conferences, media interviews and the
9/11 Commission Report.

Condi Rice carried an especially heavy load in the president's defense,
probably because she's very good at it. Her testimony to the 9/11
Commission went on the record and she was sent out the most often
to make the president's case in public.

President Bush and Vice President spoke to the 9/11 panel in tandem,
but in private and not under oath. Their statements are paraphrased in
the 9/11 report.

Andrew Card and Karl Rove gave their accounts of the day in several
interviews—they definitely should have chatted beforehand to coordinate
their BS.

Many accounts were culled from a variety of books authored by members
of the administration and others who were able to gain access to the president.
Bush isn't keen on press conferences or unscripted interviews, so he hon-
ored a small band of writers with his varied recollections of the tragic day.

Long time advisor Karen Hughes wrote a book called "Ten Minutes
From Normal" which glosses over the events on 9/11 and skips quickly
to September 14th.

White House press secretary Ari Fleischer, who was with the president on
9/11 and had a chance to set the record straight, wimps out and rehashes
the same old talking points in his book, "Taking Heat."

We cite a number of Rudolph Giuliani's leadership tips from his book, the
humbly titled "Leadership."

Bill Sammon, a White House correspondent for the Washington Times
and the author of several books about George Bush, including "Fighting
Back, The War on Terrorism—From Inside the Bush White House," adds
the most new Bush commentary to the 9/11 story. As a Bush advocate,
Mr. Sammon also adds his own thoughts based on his conversations with
the president. For those interested in Presidents Bush's actions and
thoughts during the 9/11 attacks, as told by the president, "Fighting Back"
and the corresponding articles in the Washington Times provide the most
detailed published account.

Others books and authors cited include Christopher Anderson with "George and Laura;" David Frum, "The Right Man;" Ronald Kessler, the author of "A Matter of Character" and Bob Woodward's "Bush at War."

You will notice that al Qaeda is spelled several different ways throughout the book. Quotes have been copied verbatim—including the spelling used by the author or speaker.

"President Bush has provided the steady,
consistent and principled leadership to bring our country
through the worst attack in our history.
His leadership on that day is central to his record,
and his continued leadership is critical to our ultimate success
against world terrorism."
–RUDOLPH GIULIANI RESPONDING IN MARCH OF 2004
TO CRITICISM OF BUSH'S DECISION TO USE IMAGES OF GROUND ZERO
AND 9/11 CARNAGE IN POLITICAL COMMERCIALS.

Rudy is right. George Bush's leadership on 9/11 is central to his record. Too bad too few people know the truth about that so-called leadership.

The Attacks

CHAPTER 1

Another Day, Another Photo-Op

8:14–8:55 AM
41 Minutes

"The most solemn duty of the American President is to protect the American people."
—GEORGE W. BUSH

"The nation was unprepared."
—9/11 COMMISSION REPORT

The president woke up at the Colony Beach & Tennis Resort in Sarasota, Florida on the morning of September 11, 2001. He was in the state to promote his policies on education and Sarasota was the next stop.

As Bush went about his morning routine and prepared for a ride to the Booker Elementary School for a photo-op, snipers watched from the hotel roof flanked by surface-to-air missiles. A Coast Guard vessel patrolled off shore[1] and an "AWACS" Airborne Warning and Control System plane flew overhead.

Meanwhile, in the skies to the north where the defenses were less robust, terrorists began to commandeer planes.

8:14 AM

Pilots of American Airlines Flight 11, which left Boston 15 minutes earlier for Los Angeles, fail to respond to instructions from a Boston Center air traffic controller to climb to 35,000 feet. The 9/11 Commission estimates the airliner was taken over at this time.

Only A Tradititional Hijacking Was Suspected

Cardigans, cocoa and then cocktails in Cuba—woo hoo!

"To the degree that hijacking was an issue, it was traditional hijacking."

—Dr. Condoleezza Rice
National Security Advisor
May 16, 2002

8:19 AM

"I think we're getting hijacked."

—Betty Ong,
a Flight 11 attendant, speaking on phone to American Airline officials.[2]

8:20 AM

Betty Ong reports that two flight attendants have been stabbed.

8:21 AM

The transponder of the Flight 11 aircraft is turned off.

8:24 AM

"Nobody move. Everything will be okay. If you try to make any moves, you'll endanger yourself and the airplane. Just stay quiet."[3]

—A TRANSMISSION FROM FLIGHT 11
HEARD AT BOSTON CENTER AIR TRAFFIC CONTROL.

Traditional Hijacking And Kidnapping Mentioned

Al Qaeda rarely turn violent— they're sweetie pies that way.

"It mentioned hijacking, but hijacking in the traditional sense, and in a sense, said that the most important and most likely thing was that they would take over an airliner, holding passengers and demand the release of one of their operatives."

—DR. RICE,
TALKING ABOUT THE PRESIDENT'S
AUGUST 6, 2001 DAILY BRIEF

8:37:52 AM

The military—Northeast Air Defense Sector (NEADS) is notified of the hijacking by the FAA.

FAA: Hi. Boston Center TMU [Traffic Management Unit], we have a problem here. We have a hijacked headed towards New York, and we need you guys to, we need someone to scramble some F-16's or something up there, help us out.

NEADS: Is this real-world or exercise?

FAA: No, this is not an exercise, not a test.[4]

People Might Try Hijacking Says Rice
Violent deranged people—but it's a little strong to call them terrorists

"I think it's a little strong to actually call it intelligence—the interpretation that was there that these were people who might try hijacking."

—CONDI RICE,
SPEAKING OF THE AUGUST 6, 2001 PDB

8:39 AM

President Bush's motorcade leaves the hotel and heads to the Booker Elementary School. No one in the traveling party or at the White House is aware of the hijacking.

8:42 AM

United Airlines Flight 175 makes last communication to the ground—probable time of hijacking.

Rice: Terrorists Might Blow Up A Plane

Boom, it's over—hardly worth mentioning

"All of this reporting about hijacking was about traditional hijacking. You take a plane—people were worried they might blow one up, but they were mostly worried that they might try to take a plane and use it for release of the blind Sheikh or some of their own people."

—CONDI RICE,
PRESS BRIEFING MAY 16, 2002

8:46 AM

Two fighter jets are scrambled from Otis Air Force Base in Massachusetts to track down Flight 11, as is the protocol.

Even if the jets can get to the airliner before it reaches New York, the pilots will have few options, since the president is the only person who can order the shoot-down of a commercial airliner and he's clueless.

Rice: Hijacking And Terrorism Might Be Linked

Advisor finally grasps hidden meaning in reports warning of hijackings by terrorists

"But, you know, again, that terrorism and hijacking might be associated is not rocket science."

—CONDI RICE, MAY 16, 2002

8:46:40 AM

American Airlines Flight 11 Smashes Into The North Tower Of The World Trade Center

Flying in at an angle at 450 mph, the plane rips through seven floors.[5]

Hundreds are killed instantly, including all 92 people on board the aircraft. Jet fuel ignites and a ball of fire shoots from the building and roars down elevator shafts and explodes out into floors below.

8:47 AM

The transponder code changed twice within a minute period and government authorities become suspicious of United Airlines Flight 175, which left Boston for Los Angeles at 8:14 am.[6]

George Bush is still in the limo on the way to the Booker Elementary School. He daydreams about all the brush he cleared last month in Texas and watches the tantalizing Florida-style brush fly by the tinted windows. The president sighs, and wonders what lucky duck will get to chop down the tangled thicket by one of the poor people shacks near the road.

By this time, one plane is a confirmed hijacking, one is suspect and a plane has crashed into a New York skyscraper. Authorities aren't sure which particular aircraft hit the World Trade Center.

In New York City—Thousands of people head toward the World Trade Center to help with the crisis. Some are on-duty policeman, fireman and emergency workers, others off-duty first responders and many are civilians.

8:47:50 AM

In New York City—"We have a number of floors on fire. It looked like the plane was aiming toward the building."[7]

—BATTALION FIRE CHIEF JOSEPH PFEIFER "102 MINUTES"

Not My Job Says Rumsfeld

Imaginary loophole gives terrorists free pass through U.S. airspace— Americans encouraged to install surface-to-air missile batteries on backyard patio next to Weber grill

"Under our Constitution, under our laws, the United States military's task is to defend against foreign invasion and foreign threats. The threat we saw recently was from a person in our country in one of our airplanes filled with our citizens. This is a law enforcement job. It is a job for the FBI. It is a job for the police."[8]

—DONALD RUMSFELD
INTERVIEW FOR ABC NEWS
"THIS WEEK" WITH SAM DONALDSON
SEPTEMBER 16, 2001

8:48 AM

CNN reports that a large commercial jet has crashed into the middle of one of the World Trade Center towers. Evidently, no televisions or radios are turned on in the presidential limousine, and no one has the guts to call the vehicle and interrupt Bush with the bad news during his car ride.

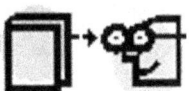

"The Department Of Defense Will Provide Military Assistance to the lead federal agency and/or the CONPLAN primary agencies during all aspects of a terrorist incident upon request by the appropriate authority and approval by the Secretary of Defense."

—"CONPLAN" OR THE "UNITED STATES GOVERNMENT INTERAGENCY DOMESTIC TERRORISM CONCEPT OF OPERATIONS PLAN"

8:52 AM

A flight attendant on board Flight 175 [second airliner to hit WTC] tells officials on the ground that the plane has been hijacked.[9]

In New York City—To escape the fire raging in the North Tower, people jump to their deaths from more than 1000 feet.

Live on ABC—Acknowledging that the cause of the crash is unknown; Diane Sawyer recalls the 1993 terrorist attack on the World Trade Center.

8:54 AM

Heading west, American Airlines Flight 77 [Pentagon bound] makes an unauthorized turn to the south.[10]

Two hijackings of commercial planes have been confirmed, another hijacking is suspected, and a large aircraft has crashed into the World Trade Center. CNN reported the first attack six minutes ago, but the Commander-in-Chief with the best telecommunications equipment at his finger tips remains ignorant.

Rumsfeld Upset With Hijackers

Can't they do anything right? complains the Secretary

"The purpose of a hijack is to take the plane from one place to another place where it wasn't intended to be going, not to fly it into buildings."

—DONALD RUMSFELD TO 9/11 PANEL
MARCH 23, 2004

Live on most television networks, the enormity of the damage caused by the first attack can be seen as flames and smoke come out of a gigantic hole high up the north tower.

8:55 AM

Clueless, But Punctual—And Crispy

Bush arrives at school nine minutes after the first attack. "We're on time. I like to stay on time; I like to be crisp."[11]

Let's Review

Four separate groups of terrorists board four different planes.

By 8:55 am, when the president reaches the school, three of the aircraft have been hijacked and a plane has crashed into the World Trade Center.

The president hasn't been informed about the World Trade Center, the hijackings or the scrambled fighter jets. Not even a postcard. Millions of people learn about the crash seven minutes before George Bush simply by watching TV.

The hijackings started 41 minutes ago and it's been nine minutes since Flight 11 smashed into the north tower. Images of the carnage are being transmitted live on television and terrorism has been mentioned as a possible cause. Will the president be able to deduce what's going on by calling the Federal Aviation Administration and the Pentagon, watching TV and drawing upon his knowledge of recent threats? Will he be able to suck it up and defend the country from further attacks?

CHAPTER 2

Bush Draws
A Blank

8:55–9:02 AM
7 Minutes

"No Alarm Bells" [1]
—GEORGE BUSH

*"I think when information came in about the first crash,
I think the natural reaction was, was it a plane that went
off course, what could this be, is this terrorism?"* [2]
—ARI FLEISCHER, WHITE HOUSE PRESS SECRETARY,
TO REPORTERS ON 9/11/2001

*"One facet of making decisions involves knowing how to
act when there's not much time to deliberate."* [3]
—RUDOLPH W. GIULIANI "LEADERSHIP"

Many Americans remember clearly the moment they heard the first
World Trade Center tower had been struck, and so does the president—
he just has a greater variety of memories than most people. And his staff
has trouble getting their stories straight, too.

It shouldn't be difficult for this dream team of public servants to recall who
told Bush about the incident and when, but they had a problem—how do
you explain nothing? How do you tell the American people that George
Bush did nothing after hearing about an airliner full of people ramming
into a landmark building full of people in the nation's largest city? Mostly,
you lie.

The straight shooter and his disciples have numerous and conflicting recollections of the moment, but there is one common thread. No way, no how, did a commercial airliner hitting the World Trade Center raise a smidgeon of suspicion in George Bush's brain—and make sure to mention that "at first" you thought it was a small plane, even if you found out it was a commercial airliner only a moment later.

Of course, months and years after 9/11, the president could say anything without getting any push-back from the interviewer. "I understand you were perched on the wing of Air Force One swatting at the terrorists with your sinewy and tastefully bronzed six iron swinging left arm? How did that go Mr. President, my lord sir—was it harrowing? Were you steadfast and manly as usual?"

In fact, most of the media was satisfied to ignore the events and time before Bush was told about the second plane crashing into the South Tower. Like the version pitched in the movie, "DC 9/11: Time of Crisis," the president's day didn't start until Andrew Card whispered sweet nothings into his ear at five minutes after 9 am as he sat in the Sarasota classroom.

But, the day started well before that moment, and if the president was unaware of the hijackings and the scrambling of Air Force jets to that point, then so be it. But certainly he was informed of the first crash into the North Tower at 8:55 am according to the 9/11 Commission—seven full minutes before he entered the classroom. At five minutes to nine, the president spoke with National Security Advisor Condi Rice and she told him a commercial airliner hit the World Trade Center. Bush then proceeds to do nothing. Seven minutes later, at 9:02 am, Bush entered the school room for a photo-op.

These are their first attack stories...

The 9/11 Commission

See No Evil:

Commercial Plane Hits Skyscraper— Thousands In Immediate Danger

National Security Advisor and President Bush less informed than viewers of Fox News

> *8:55 am: Before entering the classroom, the President spoke to National Security Advisor Condoleezza Rice, who was at the White House. She recalled first telling the President it was a twin-engine aircraft, then that it was commercial, saying "that's all we know right now, Mr. President."*

> —9/11 COMMISSION

Human resources snafu:

National Security Advisor? Maybe not a good fit for Dr. Rice. Condi went back to her regular schedule and was on time for the nine o'clock staff meeting—probably to jabber about some boring national security issue. She might make a fine Secretary of State, though.

Blissfully ignorant:

Planes aren't hijacked every day and fighter planes aren't scrambled for laughs. The president and all of the president's men and women are out of the loop and they seemed to be satisfied to stay that way.

Must see TV:

Take a break already, Ms. Rice— you're working way too hard. Put your feet up—maybe watch a little CNN with that nice Aaron Brown fellow. Here, have a nice warm Rice Crispy bar.

"We also had been getting some intelligence hits throughout the summer—mainly focused overseas, by the way—and there had been a series of responses that we took to harden embassies and it was clear that bin Laden felt emboldened and didn't feel threatened by the United States."[4]

> —GEORGE BUSH

Call waiting:
Busy signal? Forget the number? Scared? Why not call the president with news of the crash earlier, while he was cruising in the limo? Has George been monkeying around with those 976 numbers again and tying up the line?

The President

No Biggie:

Chief Of Staff Tells President Of Crash
And yada, yada, yada—thousands are dead

> *"And Andy Card says, 'By the way, an aircraft flew into the World Trade Center.'"* [5]

—GEORGE BUSH

Inflection infection:
The communication was so casual; Bush couldn't be expected to interpret the level of importance. Killer whales have the same problem—which is why they sometimes get their signals mixed up and occasionally bite off the head of the guy on the ladder with the mackerel in his mouth.

Ho hum:
How big of a building has to get rammed by a commercial plane to get Bush's attention? We don't know, yet.

> "This has bin Laden all over it, I've got to go." [6]
>
> —CIA CHIEF GEORGE TENET'S REACTION, AFTER HEARING ABOUT THE FIRST ATTACK.

On February 26, 1993, a huge bomb was detonated by terrorists in the parking garage of the north tower of the World Trade Center.

❖ ❖ ❖

He's Delirious
From The Town Hall Fever

Bush Views Crash Personally:
Turns out to be a flashback from Nam—or Mardi Gras '83

Question, From 3rd Grader Jordan:
How did you feel when you heard about the terrorist attack?

George Bush:
"I was sitting outside the classroom waiting to go in, and I saw an airplane hit the tower—the TV was obviously on. And I used to fly, myself, and I said, well, there's one terrible pilot. I said it must have been a horrible accident. But I was whisked off there. I didn't have much time to think about it."

—GEORGE BUSH, AT A TOWN HALL MEETING, IN ORLANDO, FLORIDA, DECEMBER 6, 2001

Yeah, that's it:

Not even close, George. Holy Hughes, there's barely a truthful word in the paragraph. He'll go to hell for lying to a child—Karl! The president needs rebornin' agin!

No whisking:

Bush found out about the crash seven minutes before he entered the classroom. A healthy feller like him could walk about a mile in that time, if he didn't stop to gather ticks for his collection of blood-sucking critters. Karl is the biggest, so far.

Acid?

Bush didn't see the plane hit the first tower before going into the classroom—the recording wasn't televised until later. He tells this lie at least twice.

> "Until we know what this is, Dick, we should assume the worse."[7]
>
> —Lisa Gordon-Hagerty, from the Office of Emergency Response to Richard Clarke

Why lie?

Because the president had seven minutes to contemplate and get information about an airliner hitting a building with possibly tens of thousands of people inside, the scrambled jets and the other hijackings, and decided it wasn't important enough to mess up his beloved schedule. Plus, it's just what he does. It's like his thing or something.

Poor Jordan:

He probably doesn't know it, but this is the last time the kid will be able to speak to the president, due to the "I've already met with that crazy Sheehan bitch before" Doctrine, which allows only one meeting per citizen with King George, unless you have enough money to pay for the royal privilege. No Abramoff loot or post-dated checks, please.

Spin One For The Gipper

President First Told Plane Was A Light Twin Engine
Said he knew some "light twins" in Dallas once…heh, heh, heh

> *"And my first reaction was—as an old pilot—how could the guy have gotten so off course to hit the towers? What a terrible accident that is. The first report I heard was a light airplane, twin-engine airplane."*[8]

—GEORGE BUSH

Writing history wrong:
At 8:55 am, Rice told Bush that a commercial airliner hit the World Trade Center, but the president figures that mentioning a slightly earlier conversation will make the situation appear retroactively less urgent. It's a deceitful recollection at best. Bush knows an accident caused by a heart attack or pilot error is virtually impossible in a commercial aircraft with multiple pilots.

It was so teeny:
The plane probably bounced off the huge strong building and floated gently to the ground, killing only a few elitist east coast pedestrians with pre-9/11 mentalities.

Issues Smissues… I Ordered My Bacon Crispy!

> *"I remember very well that the president was aware that there were issues inside the United States. He talked to people about this. But I don't remember the al Qaida cells as being something that we were told we needed to do something about."*

—CONDI RICE TO 9/11 COMMISSION

Cavernous:
The images on TV showed a World Trade Center tower with more than a small dent.

Why all the bad vibes?
The president is right to be unconcerned. How many pounds of explosives can a small plane possibly carry?

Walk Like An Egyptian

Rove Leaks Information Of Crash To President
Then knees him in the groin for fun

> *Rove says the cause of the crash was unclear. Bush replies,*
> *"What a horrible accident!" Bush also suggests the pilot may*
> *have had a heart attack.* [9]

—9/11 REPORT

Binary:
Glossy or matte. Accident or intentional—two choices.

Touch someone:
No need to speculate, George. Reach out—call the FAA or the dudes with all the exploding stuff.

Hughes concurs:
"And so, of course, my immediate thought was what a terrible accident, but you know, the pilot must have gotten sick or had a heart attack or a terrible accident." [11]

"I think my job is to stay ahead of the moment." [10]

—GEORGE BUSH

Laura too:
"What a weird, freak accident, Laura thought." [12]

And Condi:
"And I thought what a strange accident."

There's one joker at every attack:
But Dick, how could thou have forsaken the golden child and ruin the scripted choreography by posing the question, *"How the hell could a plane hit the World Trade Center?"* [13]

Dr. Condoleeza Rice
National Security Advisor

While Visions Of
Piper Cubs Danced In Her Head

Rice Assumes Accident
And it was strange, very strange—oh well, back to work

> *"And I thought what a strange accident. And my mind
> immediately went to a small plane of some kind, and in fact,
> the first reports were that they were small—here was some sort
> of small plane or maybe a twin-engine plane of some kind. And
> I picked up the phone and I called the President, who was in
> Florida for an education event, and he had just heard. And I said,
> "Yes, Mr. President, a plane has hit the World Trade Center." And
> he also said, 'What a strange accident.' And I said I would get
> back in touch with him later."* [14]

—CONDI RICE 9/11/2002

Repressed memory:
Later, in front of the 9/11 Commission, Rice recalled telling Bush it was a commercial plane during this very same phone call. Of course, she had a few years to ponder the conversation—and the "under oath" thing—which frightened her about the width of a dime.

Polly want a cabinet position?
Was it small? When Rice is given a talking point, she'll run with it for decades. People with the disgrace gland removed can do this effortlessly without any sense of embarrassment—well past the point of suicidal shame for a normal human.

In May 2001, the CIA tells Bush al Qaeda has shown signs of increased activity and that the group might try to hijack U.S. airliners. [15]

Blinders:
Turn your head, but don't cough. Look at the pictures on the TV. Fire, smoke—huge hole.

What a fool believes:
First reports said sunny—so I walked around in the rain for an hour, and it was very confusing.

Karl Rove
Advisor To The President

Look Kids...A Talking Weasel

Rove Tells Bush About First Attack At 8:49 AM
Advisor instructed to call Brownie, and that other fella—the fat dude from the barbeque

> *"Well, when the first plane hit, we were standing outside Emma Booker Elementary School in Sarasota, Florida. The President was literally shaking hands in the receiving line, the principal, superintendent, and so forth and myself, and it was my assistant, Susan Ralston and this was about literally 8:49, 8:50, and she said that a plane hit, struck the World Trade Center, and it was unclear whether it was a military, a commercial, whether it was a prop or a jet. So I went over and told the President."* [16]

—KARL ROVE

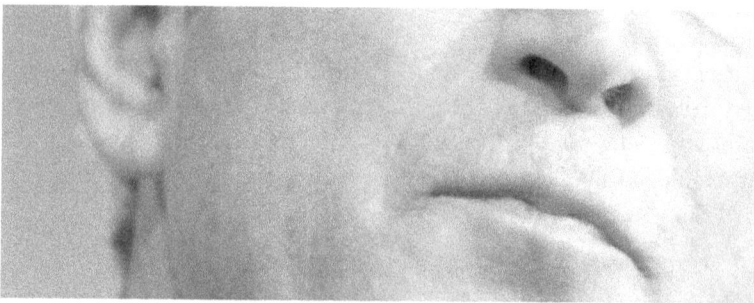

Liar:
The motorcade, equipped with the finest communication equipment, was in route to the Booker Elementary School when the airliner hit the Trade Center tower. They were in Florida, though. That was true.

Motive:
Give the impression that the president wasn't sitting in the limo reading a comic book for nine minutes after the first attack like an ignorant dork. Well done.

Two CIA analysts in preparing the August 6, 2001 President's Daily Brief believed it represented an opportunity to communicate their view that the threat of a bin Laden attack in the United States remained both current and serious.[17]

—9/11 COMMISSION REPORT

❖ ❖ ❖

Telegraph Wires Cut... Probably Varmints

Rove: We Tried To Get Information
But Novak wasn't answering his phone—out getting even larger teeth installed

> *"And then just a few moments later, 2 or 3 minutes later, Condi Rice called, but, again, there was at that point no knowledge of what it was and so forth. And we went around the corner. The President met some more people and then went into a reading drill, and those—some of the staff went next door. Wherever the President travels, there is a staff room, and so we went into the staff room next to this, I guess, first or second grade classroom in which he was. And there were telephones, secure telephones. So we began trying to get some information."*[18]

—KARL ROVE

Excellent adventure:
Karl and George went around the corner and time lurched forward seven minutes—without benefit of a souped up DeLorean.

Crackerjack staff:
Nobody called the FAA or the Defense Department, but three reserved tee times and one staffer phoned in an order to Lands End. Mostly, they stood there and gawked at the TV.

Andrew Card
White House Chief Of Staff

Andrew Card And
The Case Of The Missing Minutes

Bush Poised To Enter Classroom When Told Of First Attack

Then, an intense low pressure system literally sucks the president into the room—no one could have predicted it

> *"We were in the—in the holding room outside of a classroom. The president was getting ready to go in and meet with students to talk about reading, and word came from the situation room that there had been a plane crash into one of the World Trade Center towers. And the president was informed by Karl Rove. We were standing just as the president was getting ready to go into the classroom."* [19]

—ANDY CARD, WHITE HOUSE CHIEF OF STAFF

Lie:
Bush learned of the crash at least seven minutes before entering the classroom. To disappear the time, Card tells a lie to poor naïve Brian Williams.

Flip flop:
Card takes the opposite tack of Karl and pushes the time table forward; his story has the president learning of the first attack 13 minutes after the time Rove has stated and seven minutes after the time concluded by the 9/11 Commission.

> "It's such a beautiful day. A plane doesn't just hit the World Trade Center by accident."[20]
>
> —RUDOLPH GIULIANI "LEADERSHIP"

Card time:
Like dog years, one "Card Minute" equals seven minutes in human time.

On August 6, 2001, Bush receives a briefing from the CIA saying that al Qaeda is interested in hijacking U.S. commercial airliners.

Ari Fleischer
White House Press Secretary

Let Me Lie To You While The Events Are Still Fresh In My Mind

President Arrived At School Shortly Before 9:00
Actual time not important—we don't discuss internal time keeping methods

"The President arrived just shortly before 9:00 a.m., at the elementary school in Sarasota, when Andy Card informed him, as the President finished shaking hands in a hallway of school officials, about the crash of the first plane into the World Trade Center.

The President then proceeded directly into his hold and spoke with Dr. Condoleezza Rice, who provided him with that information, as well. The President then went before you all, in the public event, for the first event with the small children. And during the course of his speech to the—his remarks to the children, Andy Card was notified about the crash of the second airplane." [21]

—Ari Fleischer 9/11/2001

Ari time:

If a person didn't know better, they would think the president walked from the limo, took a short call from Dr. Rice and proceeded into the classroom. A surgical fleischerrific disposal of seven minutes.

Whistleblower:

Ari, are you calling Andy and Karl liars? It's OK—we just want to know.

"The system was blinking red. By late July it could not get any worse."

—CIA Director
George Tenet to 9/11 Commission

Fleischer Facts...
Like Factual Facts, Only Less So

NO ONE Knew It Was A Terrorist Attack

And that means "nobody"...unless you want Karl and Scooter rooting through your trash

"In the initial minutes after the first tower was hit, there was little to report. No one yet knew it was a terrorist attack..."[22]

—ARI FLEISCHER

Lie:
The FAA and the United States Air Force had plenty to report. The networks were using the words, "possibly terrorism." Slacks on fire.

A known known:
Not many people "knew" it was terrorism, but plenty had common sense concerns, including Fleischer. On 9/11 he said, *"I think the natural reaction was, was it a plane that went off course, what could this be, is this terrorism?"*[24]

"In June and July when the threat spikes where so high...we were at battle stations."[23]

—NATIONAL SECURITY ADVISER CONDOLEEZZA RICE, MARCH 22, 2004

Wordplay?
How long do the initial minutes last? In George Bush's case—at least 18. A dozen is now 89.

8:58 AM

"We might have a hijack over here, two of them."

—NEW YORK CENTER CONTROLLER

Karen Hughes
Advisor To The President

We All Believe
Tobacco To Be Non-Addictive

Karen Hughes Reads Minds
And when she reads your mind, it stays read

> *"Condi Rice had talked to the president just after they arrived at the school in Florida, but they didn't know any more than I did. They all assumed it was some kind of weird accident; at that point terrorism didn't occur to us."*[25]

—KAREN HUGHES "TEN MINUTES FROM NORMAL"

Cheap trick:
Hughes has no idea what everyone assumed and it isn't relevant. The president isn't excused for being equally naïve.

Mushroom cloud:
You "all" assumed it was a weird accident—didn't you? Say it, Condi! Say it! Say it! OK—very nice. Now say, "he gassed his own people" 8,000 times in a row.

> *"He [Bush] said a commercial plane has hit the World Trade Center, and we're going to go ahead and go on, we're going on to do the reading thing anyway."*[26]
>
> —BOOKER SCHOOL PRINCIPAL
> GWEN TOSE'-RIGELL

From January 20th through September 10th, the president received more than 40 briefing items on al-Qaida.[27]

8:59 AM

In New York City—Caution

Port Authority Police Department Sgt. Al DeVona orders evacuation of World Trade Center Complex, "…until we find out what caused it."[28]

—"102 MINUTES"

9:00 AM

On Flight 175, "passenger Brian David Sweeney called his mother and told her that his flight had been hijacked. He said the passengers were thinking of storming the cockpit to wrest control of the plane away from the hijackers."

—9/11 COMMISSION REPORT

"Bin Laden Determined To Strike in US"
Title of the President's August 6, 2001 Daily Brief

9:01 AM

"We have several situations going on here. It's escalating big, big time. We need to get the military involved with us."[29]

—MANAGER AT THE FAA'S NEW YORK CENTER

9:02 AM

Bush decides nothing requires his attention and he enters the classroom.

Let's Review

8:55-9:02 am

Multiple hijackings have been detected, the World Trade Center has been attacked and the Air Force has scrambled fighter jets. Hundreds of people have died from the crash and thousands more are in danger from the fire and falling debris. The president remains in the dark about the hijackings and the actions of the military.

Karl Rove says the president was already at the Booker Elementary School when the plane struck the north tower at 8:46 am.

Bill Sammon of the Washington Times claims that Bush arrived at school at 8:55 am.

Ari Fleischer recalls the motorcade pulling up to the school "shortly" before 9:00 am.

The 9/11 Commission says that Bush was inside the school talking to Rice at 8:55 am—nine minutes after the attack and 7 minutes after TV audiences heard the news. The hijackings started 41 minutes before at 8:14 am.

Andy Card claims that Bush was told by Karl Rove about the first attack moments before the president entered the classroom at 9:02 am.

Karl said he told the president about the first attack at 8:49 am. Bush said that Andy Card told him.

The president also said that he saw the first plane hit the World Trade Center on television and then was "whisked" into the classroom.

Less than 15 minutes after being hijacked, passengers aboard Flight 175 are making plans to fight their captors. After hearing that a commercial airliner has hit the World Trade Center, George Bush decides that a photo-op is the most important use of his time.

The level of destruction caused by the airliner can be seen clearly on television. There is a huge hole in the building along with fire and a tremendous amount of smoke.

Television commentators are saying the cause of the crash is unknown, that it could be an accident or intentional. The word terrorism is used, as well as references to the 1993 World Trade Center bombing orchestrated by al Qaeda.

At the very least Bush knew...
- Al Qaeda cells were inside the United States.
- Intelligence indicated the possibility of hijackings by al Qaeda.
- Landmark and government buildings are always primary targets.
- The World Trade Center had been bombed by al Qaeda in 1993.
- Terrorists had sworn to bring the World Trade Center down.
- Al Qaeda was a topic in 40 of his daily briefs.
- Planes could be used as weapons due to his experience at the G-8 summit in July 2001 and watching WWII movies.
- He put everyone at battle stations earlier that summer.

And yet—no alarm bells for President Bush?

"I don't give a damn for a man who is not always on his toes."
—GENERAL PATTON D-DAY SPEECH

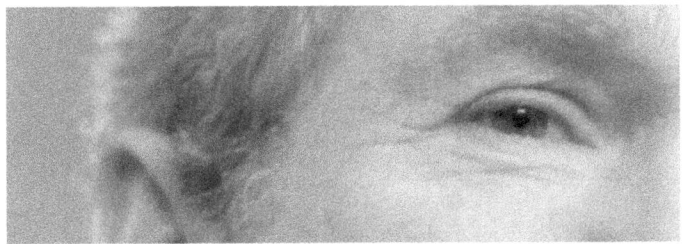

CHAPTER THREE

Pondering Disaster
Attack Number 2

9:03–9:12 AM
9 Minutes

9:03:11 AM

United Airlines Flight 175 Crashes Into The South Tower Of The World Trade Center

At more than 500 mph,
the airliner cuts through the 77th through 85th floors.

"The need for quick decisions, of course, is strongest in times of crisis. People are afraid and uncertain, and need to feel that someone is in charge." [1]
—RUDOLPH GIULIANI "LEADERSHIP"

Unsurprisingly, the president is sitting on his ass when the second tower is hit. Deciding that a commercial airliner hitting just one of the Trade Center towers didn't rise to a presidential bother and unable to sweet talk his own government into sharing news of the hijacked planes and scrambled fighter jets, Bush has gone on with his precious photo-op.

It will take a couple of minutes before the Chief of Staff gathers the guts to interrupt the photogenic president with the latest attack update and another seven minutes on his bum for Bush to mull it over.

Of course, Bush's people are sure to mention that terrorism never entered any of their minds until the second attack—and then, boing! Wow, this is terrorism. I guess those al Qaeda guys weren't kidding. Quick! Round up Cat Stevens and start reading up on this terrorism thing.

9:03 AM

Attack In Last Throes

Second Plane Crash
Triggers Suspicion Of Terrorism
Cheney awarded honorary MENSA membership

> *"So we turned on the television and watched for a few minutes, and then actually saw the second plane hit the World Trade Center. And the—as soon as that second plane showed up, that's what triggered the thought: terrorism, that this was an attack..."*[2]

—DICK CHENEY ON MEET THE PRESS SEPTEMBER 16, 2001

Defense mastermind:
HE's the brains of this outfit? No wonder Scooter was able to operate right under VP's nose.

For Chalabi's eyes only:
Now we know. A super prime high quality terrorist target has to be hit at least twice before this White House will consider the possibility of terrorism.

Goldie sherlocks:
I can't be sure, but this giant blood stained 18 pound bowling trophy on the mantle might be the murder weapon.

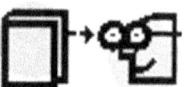

CONPLAN

"United States Government Interagency Domestic Terrorism Concept Of Operations Plan"

The complexity, scope, and potential consequences of a terrorist threat or incident require that there be a rapid and decisive capability to resolve the situation.

—PUBLISHED JANUARY 2001

No Refunds

Photo-Op In Florida
Canceled Says Hughes
Except for the part on tape—we're not sure how that got past us

> *"And my first reaction was to drop to my knees and say a prayer for our country, because I realized immediately, like everyone did, that this was no accident, this was a planned attack. And then I spent most of the next 45 minutes to an hour on the phone with the folks in Florida as you know, we cancelled the event there, and when they took off from Florida, I was under the impression they were coming back to Washington."* [3]

—KAREN HUGHES

Freedom lies:
The president sat through the reading drill and stayed at the school to give an ill-advised statement to the nation at 9:30 am, so his visit wasn't so much canceled, as interrupted. How annoying.

Rain out:
Hughes knows the event should have been canceled after the first attack, but it wasn't—so she just lies. Karen is very credible among people who have never heard her say anything.

Attention Deficit

Commercial Airliner Hits World Trade Center
National Security Advisor goes ahead with more important staff meeting

> *"I then went downstairs to the daily senior staff meeting, in which I can go around and ask all of the senior staff what's going on in their area of responsibility. And I got about three people in, and the executive assistant handed me a note and it said a second plane has hit the World Trade Center. And I thought, "My God, this is a terrorist attack."* [4]

—CONDI RICE

Peas in a pod:
For a smart person, Dr. Rice doesn't turn out to be any brighter than
the president when it comes to defense. Very embarrasing—especially for
someone with the word "security" in their job title.

Talk is cheap:
The Bush people are constantly talking about national security, campaigning
as strong on defense and tough on terrorism, but none of them are actually
prepared to do anything when the country is under attack. Yack, yack,
yack—boom—zilch.

9:04 AM

Don't "Bring 'Em On" Yet...

Chief Of Staff Deliberates
Telling President Of Attack
If you spook him, we'll never find him

> *"And then I rushed to decide how to inform the president and when to
> inform him. And the test that I went through: If I were president,
> would I want to know?"* [5]

—ANDREW CARD

Imaginary conundrum:
The Commander-in-Chief is the highest ranking person in the chain of
command. Withholding information of an attack is not an option unless
you're absolutely certain the president is a drooling idiot.

Card wash:
Andy gives the impression that any action by Bush is purely voluntary—like showing up for National Guard service.

Essence of time:
That's just great—two more minutes down the toilet. If a powerful Iraqi warship, armed with deadly aluminum tubes and toting tons of carrot cake, was just spotted sputtering in the mid Atlantic on course towards North America, we could take several days to decide whether to vaporize the mighty boat—or less dramatically blow a Volkswagen Passat size hole in the hull and let it flutter to the ocean floor like lava in a lamp. This wasn't like that.

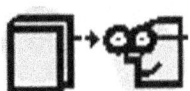

Flashback

President Puts Office Staff On Battle Stations During Summer

Had to buy own body armor, though—and playing cards with enemy faces

"We don't want to be caught unprepared. We don't want to rule out the possibility of a threat to the homeland. And therefore preparatory steps need to be made. So the president put us on battle stations." [6]

—STEVEN HADLEY
DEPUTY NATIONAL SECURITY ADVISER

❖ ❖ ❖

9:04:30 AM

Verstehen Sie?

Card Searches For Words Requiring No Explanation To President
Comes up dry—goes with regular English words and hopes for the best

"I wanted to explain the enormity of the situation without answering questions from him. I didn't want to have a discussion in front of the classroom or in front of the media. And so I tried to pick words that would succinctly describe the situation and would require no explanation." [7]

—ANDREW CARD

Wasting away in priorityville:
Card was more concerned with the perception of the media than the attack, which is standard procedure for this administration in all situations. "Perception beats reality every time"—those words are tattooed on Rove's ass next to "Valerie" and the secret recipe for Ralph Reed's Famous Double Dipper Casino Casserole.

Dubious dilemma:
The Chief of Staff was not forced to have a discussion in front of the kids or the media, evidently his worse fear. He could have whispered, "Mr. President, something pretty f_____ significant is happening and you need to come with me right now! We desperately need your competent leadership." And in his regular voice, "I'm sorry kids, but the president's jock itch is flaring up and he has to leave. This other middle aged white guy with the dopey grin will sit and listen to you read."

> ## Meanwhile, In Rummy World— Waiting For The Monthly Newsletter
>
> The secretary was informed of the 2nd strike during a briefing; he resumed the briefing while awaiting more information.
>
> —9/11 COMMISSION REPORT

❖ ❖ ❖

9:05 AM

Sir...Some Stem Cells Are In Danger!

President Bush Told "America Is Under Attack"
Well, that didn't do any good—try poking him with a pool cue

> *"I saw him coming to recognition of what I had said.*
> *I think he understood that he was going to have to take*
> *command as commander-in-chief, not just as president."*[8]

—ANDREW CARD

**Do you hear
the words coming out
of my mouth?**
Card "thinks" Bush understood.
That's as good a read on him as
you're going to get.

Wishful thinking:
Bush doesn't know he IS
Commander-in-Chief.

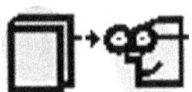

"The CONPLAN is based on the
premise that a terrorist incident
may occur at any time of day with
little or no warning, may involve
single or multiple geographic areas,
and result in mass casualties."

—United States Government
Interagency Domestic Terrorism
Concept of Operations Plan or
CONPLAN, Published January 2001

The President's
First Thoughts Upon Hearing
Of The Second Attack

*"I was thinking about what the heck we were going to do. I'm
an action-oriented guy. And I am thinking to myself: What is it I
need to do?"* [9]

—George Bush

*"...for all he knew there could have been 15 to 20 other attacks
going on. He could have been targeted there in Florida."* [10]

—Rep. Peter King,
evidently trying to help the president's case for freezing

When Andy Card whispered into Bush's ear, "America is under attack," he may as well have asked him to perform a kidney transplant or play the banjo. The chances were zero the president would know what to do, since he never got past the fundraising, perpetual campaigning, photo-ops and vacation chapters in the assigned reading.

And, even though one World Trade Center tower was hit 19 minutes before, the president has evidently erased any lingering thoughts on that topic and now his brain must reboot and start again from the beginning. There's no problem in George's mind, though—because like many others with an over developed sense of self esteem, Bush just assumed he naturally possessed the instincts required to handle any situation—he would simply bullshit his way out of any mess that popped up.

Charm and connections might have worked with the SEC and the Texas Air National Guard, but unfortunately for the country, actual knowledge was needed for this crisis.

The president had nearly 20 minutes since the first attack to figure out what was going on, but most American's are under the impression that Bush had no reason to know anything about the attacks until Andrew Card breaks the news to him at 9:05 am. According to the fable, the day of 9/11 doesn't start for the president until he hears about the second attack, so understandably, questions mostly from adoring fans, asking about Bush's first thoughts after Card whispers in his ear were plentiful. And, as is Bush administration custom, the varieties of responses were abundant, too.

If the truth won't play well to the hand-picked crowds, fictional accounts will do—and if the first few stories don't poll well, try something new.

❖ ❖ ❖

Bush Glued To Chair With Elmers Young Pranksters Sent To Gitmo

Card Abandons President
Bush held hostage by second graders—some bigger than average with muttonchops

"Then he left. There was no time for discussion or anything." [11]

That's typical:
They never set aside enough time at these meetings to hear what's on the mind of the little people, some who may be immobilized by fright.

In New York City— Americans Put Fears On Hold And Take Action

Regular citizens jump from the crowd and help direct traffic to clear the way for emergency vehicles to get to the burning World Trade Center buildings.

That Does It...Get My Flight Suit

Bush: We're Going To War!
But, I can't do it now—I have carpal tunnel and a cyst on my Delay

> *"They had declared war on us, and I made up my mind at that moment that we were going to war."* [12]

—GEORGE BUSH

Good thinking Chief:
The attacks in progress can wait.

Uh oh:
Looks like an unexpected brain breach. Totally unpredictable.

Who's The Boss?

"Most important, good organization helps assure accountability. At every level of organization, elected officials—and particularly the President as Commander-in-Chief—must be able to ascertain quickly and surely who is in charge."

—HART-RUDMAN REPORT
ON TERRORISM, JANUARY 2001

Old Rough & Ready

Bush Told Of Attack
Decides to legislate from the bench

> *"We're at war and somebody has dared attack us and we're going to do something about it. I realized I was in a unique setting to receive a message that somebody attacked us, and I was looking at these little children and all of the sudden we were at war. I can remember noticing the press pool and the press corps beginning to get the calls and seeing the look on their face. And it became evident that we were, you know, that the world had changed."* [13]

—GEORGE BUSH

Youthful indiscretion:
It's traditional to fight the terrorists over here before fighting them over there, especially when they are over here and fighting us here right now.

Geographical irrelevance:
There's no good place to learn of an attack in progress. Protecting the children and the rest of the country should have been Bush's first priority, instead of using the kids as an excuse for his paralysis.

At the ready rationalization:
The compulsory "New World" rhetoric just came to mind as

"The complexity, scope, and potential consequences of a terrorist threat or incident require that there be a rapid and decisive capability to resolve the situation."

—CONPLAN

Bush sat there bewildered. Oh my, the world just changed, and not in an evolutionary way—more like in a "quick intelligent being involved in some way" fashion, so don't look at me—I'm just as surprised as the next guy.

MEB:
Missing Empathy Bone. No concern for the dead, the dying and the about to be attacked. The useless skeletal protuberance was removed personally by good ol' Ma "they're only poor people" Bush when George was in prep school.

Hey melonhead!
Pay attention! Card didn't say the attacks were over.

❖ ❖ ❖

Weekend At Bushies

President Ponders Meaning Of Four Words
Ivy League education really paying off

> *"Andy quietly retreated, leaving the President to sit there,*
> *his face masking his emotions, pondering the meaning of*
> *those four words—America is under attack—as school children*
> *proudly read to them from their textbooks."* [14]

—ARI FLEISCHER

Excessive pondering:
Nearly two minutes per word.
No wonder he doesn't read the
newspaper.

> ### First Priority Not Masking Emotions, But Good Guess
>
> Preserving life or minimizing
> risk to health. This constitutes
> the first priority of operations.
>
> —CONPLAN

❖ ❖ ❖

Freedom Not Yet On The March

Victory
Bush toyed with idea of defending citizens from ongoing attacks—decided
against it

"Victory clicked into my mind. The one thing that became certain is that we wouldn't let this stand. I mean, there was no question in my mind that we'd respond. I wasn't sure who the attacker was. But if somebody is going to attack America, I knew that my most immediate job was to protect America by finding him and getting them." [15]

—GEORGE BUSH

Technical difficulties:
Bush's brain is stuck on fast forward again. The pictures in his head are showing arid lands with big lumpy beasts being bombed to baby powder. Please stand by.

Second Priority Of CONPLAN

Preventing a threatened act from being carried out or an existing terrorist act from being expanded or aggravated.

Big red flag:
Finding them? They're in the planes. Can somebody please check this guy for a pulse?

President Goes Into A Persistent Vegetative State—No One Notices

Bush Told, "America Is Under Attack"
Waits patiently for brain to comprehend unscripted statement

"And I can't remember anything the lady was saying from that point on. I might have been looking at her, but I wasn't hearing. And my mind was registering what it meant to hear 'America is under attack' and to be the commander in chief of the country at that moment." [16]

—GEORGE BUSH

It's only a dream:
It was like the worst, "I didn't read the book, I can't find the book, I can't find the classroom" college nightmare ever—with suicide planes in the halls.

Feelings... Whoa Whoa Whoa Feelings

"From the beginning, President Bush expressed the outrage of the American people. He immediately took charge; there was no mistaking who was commander in chief." [17]

—SEAN HANNITY EXPLAINING HOW THE PRESIDENTIAL EMOTIONS THWARTED NONE OF THE 9/11 ATTACKS.

❖ ❖ ❖

TelePrompter In The Shop

Card To President: "America Is Under Attack"
Bush not falling for that one again

Question:

One thing, Mr. President, is that you have no idea how much you've done for this country. And another thing is that, how did you feel when you heard about the terrorist attack?

George Bush:
"...and, Jordan, I wasn't sure what to think at first.
You know, I grew up in a period of time where the idea of America being under attack never entered my mind—just like your Daddy's and Mother's mind probably. And I started thinking hard in that very brief period of time about what it meant to be under attack. I knew that when I got all of the facts that we were under attact there would be hell to pay for attacking America."

—GEORGE BUSH AT A TOWN HALL MEETING IN ORLANDO, FLORIDA, DECEMBER 6, 2001

History buff...ooon:
Bush grew up during the cold war—a few thousand nuclear warheads were pointed this way. The phrase "Mutual Assured Destruction" was coined to describe the situation. He also protected the borders from an attack by the Viet Cong as a fighter pilot.

Hey, what are all these bombs for?
Half a trillion dollars is spent on defense every year. Evidently, we're suspicious of something.

Moist palms:
Oh my! What does it mean to be under attack? What does anything mean? Should I filibuster? Should I make an appointment during recess on the monkey bars?

Cold day in New Orleans:
Yes, the attackers will surely suffer a torturous afterlife when George gets the "facts" and can confirm that the country is under attack. The Chief of Staff was probably just goofing with the president when he told him, "America is under attack."

Teamwork, people!
Rove forgets to tell the president what to think. Karl gets docked one treasonous leak and dessert cart privileges for two Card weeks.

Lonesome George

Nobody To Talk To Recalls President
Staff plays prank—hides in broom closet...for like the eighth time this week

> *"I have nobody to talk to. My God, I'm Commander-in-Chief and the country has just come under attack!"* [18]

—GEORGE BUSH

Victim complex:
As usual, Bush is the aggrieved party. How inconvenient to bear so much responsibility and then have the people he relies on to cut gum out of his hair leave him all alone. Unable to cope in the unscripted setting, he frets about being the Commander-in-Chief, and then decides to do nothing.

My God:
"I'm trapped in a burning skyscraper! But, poor poor George, he's all alone and without notes."

> ## Yellowcake Removed From Bush's Spine
>
> *"First of all, a president has got to be the calcium in the backbone. If I weaken, the whole team weakens. If I'm doubtful, I can assure you there will be a lot of doubt."* [19]
>
> —GEORGE BUSH

"You can't let yourself be paralyzed by any situation."

—RUDOLPH GIULIANI "LEADERSHIP"

Not Interested In Lawyers Except For James Baker And Matlock

Thought Of Attack Amazing
Thought of defending country coming soon—after 17 more meetings and a light brunch

> *"And in the meantime, this teacher was going on about the curriculum, and I was thinking about what it meant for America to be under attack. It was an amazing thought. But I made up my mind that if America was under attack, we'd get them. I wasn't interested in lawyers, I wasn't interested in a bunch of debate. I was interested in finding out who did it and bringing them to justice. I also knew that they would try to hide, and anybody who provided haven, help, food, would be held accountable by the United States of America."*

—GEORGE BUSH AT A JANUARY 5, 2002 TOWN HALL MEETING IN ONTARIO, CA

He's not kidding:
He really did just sit there thinking about what it meant.

Play to the base:
Cheap lawyer bashing—always a crowd pleaser. And, "how about those intellectual elitist guys— who put the Rove encrusted horseshoe in their bean dip? Is this mic on? But seriously…"

Extreme manliness:
No lawyers, no debate, no clue— just a pinch between the cheek and gum.

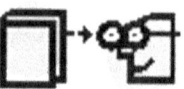

We Have A Policy

It is the policy of the United States to deter, defeat and respond vigorously to all terrorist attacks on our territory and against our citizens, or facilities, whether they occur domestically, in international waters or airspace or on foreign territory.

—PRESIDENTIAL DIRECTIVE 39, 1995

Bush Doctrine born:
Includes all guilty countries, except for ▉▉▉▉▉▉ and, ▉▉▉▉▉ and maybe ▉▉▉▉▉ .

❖ ❖ ❖

Stings Like A Butterfly
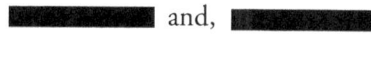

Bush Action Orientated Guy
But he can go either way—not that there's anything wrong with that

> *"I was thinking about what the heck we were going to do. I'm an action-oriented guy. And I am thinking to myself: What is it I need to do?"* [20]

—GEORGE BUSH

What a jackass:
Bush had time for a month-long vacation after a grueling six months in office, but couldn't squeeze in a few hours to learn his duties in a crisis. The only person in the country who can order the shoot down of a commerical airliner is the president, but the president doesn't know it.

National Defense Is First Talking Point

"As I said in speech after speech, education is for a state what national defense is for the federal government, the first priority and most urgent challenge."

—GEORGE W. BUSH
"A CHARGE TO KEEP" 1999

The Vice President Tries To Help

Kool And The Gang

**VP Brings In Condi,
Scooter And Mary For Discussion**
Judith Miller and dozens of generals wait patiently for their thoughts

*"National security adviser, my chief of staff, Scooter Libby,
Mary Matalin, who works for me, convened in my office, and we
started talking about getting the Counterterrorism Task Force up
and operating."*

—DICK CHENEY ON MEET THE PRESS 9/16/2001

Jokers to the right:
Task force? Started talking about? And then Scooter said, "I'm thinking about getting the gang together and puttin' on a show!"

Gilligan And The Skipper

Cheney Summons President To Call ASAP
They've been longing for the sound of each others voice for nearly ten minutes

> *"I'd given word to Andy Card's staff, who is right next door, to get hold of Andy and/or the president and that I wanted to talk to him as soon as they could hook it up."*

> —DICK CHENEY ON MEET THE PRESS 9/16/2001

Macho Rating Drops 9 Points:
The president isn't accountable to the VP—at least not Constitutionally.

It's possible:
Maybe the president knows exactly what to do and doesn't have time to gab with the vice president. Chew on that Cheney—have some faith, man.

Waiting game:
You have to wait for Bush to get done with his photo-op, just like everyone else, Dick. In the fourth grade, he strung out his class picture session for two hours.

9:09 AM
Fighter planes at Langley Air Force Base in Hampton, Virginia are placed on battle stations.

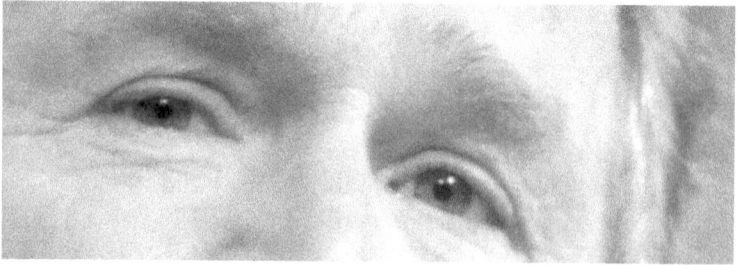

The Mayor Thanks God

I Love You, Maaan!

New York Attacked—Thousands Dead
Gotham Mayor thankful for George Bush

> *"At the time, we believed we would be attacked many more times that day and in the days that followed. Spontaneously, I grabbed the arm of then Police Commissioner Bernard Kerik and said to Bernie, 'Thank God George Bush is our President.'"*
>
> —Rudolph Giuliani at 2004 Republican Convention

Smootchy:
It's a good thing there weren't any more suicide planes coming at New York, because they would have succeeded in their mission. The president never gave the order to stop more attacks, and the mayor knows it.

> *"Rebuilding America's homeland defenses is an urgent priority."*
>
> —George W. Bush "A Charge to Keep" 1999

Review

9:03-9:12 am

The Chief of Staff decides telling the president about an ongoing attack is the right thing to do. That took two minutes.

The Commander-in-Chief knew there was something he needed to do, but he couldn't put his finger on it, so he just sat and rehearsed a list of possible first thoughts for seven minutes. He later decided they were all gems and told them all.

Vice President Cheney, the little helper, does his part to defend our country by holding a meeting.

CHAPTER FOUR

Tex, Lies And Videotape
After the pondering came the excuses...

9:05-9:12 AM
The 7 Minutes On Video Tape

"More than anyone, leaders should welcome being held accountable. Nothing builds confidence in a leader more than a willingness to take responsibility for what happens during his watch."
—RUDOLPH GIULIANI "LEADERSHIP"

Columbo

Airplanes Kill At 8:46, 9:03, 9:38 And 10:03 AM
President does everything in his power at 10:15 am—kind of

"Had I known that the enemy was going to use airplanes to kill on that fateful morning, I would have done everything in my power to protect the American people."

—GEORGE W. BUSH MAY 17, 2002

"I made the pledge to myself and to people that I'm not going to forget what happened on September 11." [1]
—GEORGE BUSH

George Bush wasted over 100 minutes during the attacks, so it was a godsend for the president that the seven minutes in the classroom turned up on video. Instead of needing to defend every chunk of time he flushed down the toilet, Bush only had to manufacture excuses for the seven minutes and, of course, his narrow escape to Louisiana and Nebraska. George Bush didn't forget 9/11—he just remembers it in many different ways. He and his apologists don't miss a possible rationalization for his classroom freeze-up.

A Kinder Gentler Defense

Bush: Instincts Took Over
Used same finely tuned senses drilling for oil in Texas—and dumping stock

> *"The President told us his instinct was to project calm, not to have the country see an excited reaction in a moment of crisis. The national press corps was standing behind the children in the classroom; he saw their phones and pagers start to ring. The President felt he should project strength and calm until he could better understand what was happening."*
>
> —9/11 COMMISSION

> *"I'm not a textbook player, I'm a gut player."* [2]
>
> —GEORGE BUSH

Fiddler:
Bush sat and did nothing while the Trade Center towers burned and planes drew a bead on other targets, and he's proud of it.

Jethro:
Terrorists or hurricanes aren't going to wait for a soft-headed leader to catch up after he's done posing.

Delusional omnipotence:
The country could not see him in real time and most people would never see the video. Evidently not considered news, taped TV showings of the president's strength and calm were rare. Millions of people had to purchase a movie ticket for the documentary Fahrenheit 9/11 to witness the presidential deportment. It was the first Pay-for-View event of a president sitting in a chair.

Girlie man:
Projection of calm saved zero lives, but al Qaeda and terrorist appeasers were happy with the president's restraint.

Claptrap:
Bush could have easily left the room and done his job minus an excited reaction. Had he done that funny walk he does all the time—the one where he pretends like he has a softball under each armpit—he would have gotten a big laugh from the physical comedy loving tykes.

Twitchy:
Whatever Bush was projecting, it wasn't strength and calm. Dr. Frist studied the tape and said the president appeared to be conscious, but possibly constipated.

❖ ❖ ❖

Mighty Mouse

Bush Knew Role As Commander-In-Chief
Responds forcefully after attacks are over—it's his trademark

> "...and so, I got on the phone from Air Force One, asking to find out the facts. You've got to understand, Jordan, during this period of time, there were all kinds of rumors floating around. Some of them were erroneous. Obviously—for example, there was a news report saying that the State Department had been attacked. I needed to know what the facts were. But I knew I needed to act. I knew that if the nation's under attack, the role of the Commander-In-Chief is to respond forcefully to prevent other attacks from happening. And so, I've talked to the Secretary of Defense; one of the first acts I did was to put our military on alert."

—GEORGE BUSH AT TOWNHALL MEETING

Crying game:
Please understand Jordan, puleeeze. I'm only a man and the facts kept coming and coming and coming. It was a blizzard, a foggy blizzard—a super foggy blizzard of endless information blowing by like...a blizzard. I was helpless, Jordan, I tell ya, it was a living hell, but a cold and blizzard-like hell. You've got to beleeeve me, Jordan!

Plastic Turkey:
Fighter planes were in the air long before Bush ever figured out who the Defense Secretary was. "The grouchy guy—you're kidding? I'm not talking to that dick."

Learning curve:
Bush didn't act. He didn't respond forcefully. Understanding his role after the attacks didn't save a single life.

Larry King Show— CNN August 12, 2004 Special 4-Part Excuse For The Seven Seated Minutes

Larry King I
Larry! The Little Bastards Were Filibustering, I Tell You!

Plenty Of Time To Defend Country Later
Politeness and pacifism are the cornerstones of our society

> *"Well, I had just been told by Andrew Card that America was under attack. And I was collecting my thoughts. And I was sitting with a bunch of young kids, and I made the decision there that we would let this part of the program finish, and then I would calmly stand up and thank the teacher and thank the children and go take care of business."*

> —GEORGE BUSH

Rewritten history
Did George go take care of business like he told Larry? Not quite. According to the 9/11 Commission, the only decision made by Bush during the 18 minutes he spent in the school holding room after leaving the classroom photo-op, was to return to D.C.—and to wear his hair up for the speech at 9:30 am.

Loitering:
"Bush lingered until an aide ushered the press out." [4]

Thin manuscript:
A collection of Bush thoughts.

Don't Start Without Me—Ask Them To Circle For A Couple Hours

"Should the military have the authority to shoot down a jet— commercial jetliner? That decision to be made by surrogates? It's a decision to be made by the president." [3]

—ANDREW CARD TO BRIAN WILLIAMS
CNBC SEPTEMBER 9, 2002

❖ ❖ ❖

Larry King II
Dumb Waiter

Bush Figures Out We Are At War
Takes a shiny medal out of petty cash—and some quarters for a Snickers bar

"And I think what's important is how I reacted when I realized America was under attack. It didn't take me long to figure out we were at war. It didn't take me long to develop a plan that we would go after al Qaeda. We went into action very quickly."

—GEORGE BUSH

Bush as a Police Officer:

"And I think what's important is how I reacted when I realized the woman was being tortured and murdered. Although I didn't try to defend her from the evildoer during the attack per se, it didn't take me more than a few hours after she died to figure out it was a crime. It didn't take me long to develop a plan that I would go after the murderer. I went into action very quickly."

Low bar:

Hey, he figured out a name for the conflict; do you expect him to do everything?

At Least Little George Is In The Majority

People caught up in disasters tend to fall into three categories. About 10% to 15% remain calm and act quickly and efficiently. Another 15% completely freak out. Most people do little. They are "stunned and bewildered."[5]

—BRITISH PSYCHOLOGIST JOHN LEACH

Delicate flower:

Good grief Larry; he wants to use 9/11 as a backdrop for his outstanding leadership—the cornerstone of his administration, but you can't expect the president to answer questions about the actual day. Softball's, my butt.

❖ ❖ ❖

Larry King III
Little Appeaser Caesar

Bush: My Actions On 9/11 Not Relevant

Choosing name for conflict most important accomplishment—it was a tossup between war or fracas

> *"What is relevant is whether or not I understand and understood then the stakes. And I recognized that we were at war. And I made a determination that we would do everything we could to bring those killers to justice and to protect the American people. That is my most solemn duty."*

> —GEORGE BUSH

Air ball:
But he didn't protect the American people. Bush seems to understand the basic concept of the "doing one's duty," but appears to be a little unclear on the follow-through.

Bush the lifeguard:
"It's not relevant that I sat by as that feller drowned. What's important is I understood that drowning is bad and recognized the dangers of water, which nobody could have foreseen. As he took his last breath and sunk like a stone, I made a determination to do everything I could to protect folks from drowning on my watch. That is my most solemn duty."

America Was Impotent Before Bush Too

"The antiseptic notion of launching a cruise missile into some guy's, you know, tent, really is a joke. I mean, people viewed that as the impotent America…a flaccid, you know, kind of technologically competent but not very tough country that was willing to launch a cruise missile out of a submarine and that'd be it." [6]

—GEORGE BUSH

Failure to engage the enemy:
Court martial for a real soldier and time in the brig.

Pompous gasbag:
George Bush decides what's relevant. Not you Larry—or that Constitution thing, written by a bunch of long haired pansies.

Larry King IV
It's A Hard Knock Life

President Seeks Meaning
Dreams of better days when the rubble grew so very tall…aaah

King:

"Wasn't that the hardest seven minutes of your life?"

Bush:

"Well, there's been a lot of hard moments in my life."

King:

"But at that moment, to hear that news…"

Bush:

"Yes, it was—trying to understand exactly what it meant. But there have been a lot of hard moments. It was hard to go to the ground zero on September the 14th, 2001, and see those workers and police men and women and the firefighters who had been searching the rubble looking for their loved ones. That was a hard moment. But it was a moment where I resolved to them publicly that we would do our duty in government, and protect this country by staying on the offense."

Dense as lead:
Trying to understand what it meant? That's what the academic types call a red flag—thanks for applying.

The old switcheroo:
Bush always moves the conversation to his rubble standing on the 14th and the subsequent attack on Afghanistan. He seems to be uncomfortable boasting about the time he kept the country from going into a panic by not standing up. It's hard to be humble.

If Time Allows

"I will never relent in defending America, whatever it takes."

—George Bush

It's been torture:
Lots of hard moments? Texas taxpayers bought him a baseball stadium—
ouch! And, once he had to fly coach and was asked to fold his shoulders in.

Slacker:
But, he'll do his duty now that he knows it's an issue, if you want to make
a federal case out of it.

How about resistance?
Can we still defend ourselves against attacks, or just do the offense?

He's a Doberman:
"And thank you so much for doing a great job this morning," Tose-Rigell
said to the children as she approached Bush. The dawdler in chief did not
even get up. [7, 8]

—BILL SAMMON "FIGHTING BACK"

"I'm ready to go. Sometimes that's the way I am—fiery." [9]

—GEORGE BUSH

And They Make Great Human Shields If You Bend Down Far Enough

Bartlett:
President's Instinct Not To Frighten Children
Wait until the kids in Baghdad get a load of shock & awe

Whitehouse spokesman Dan Bartlett said that as the president's
staff was trying to learn more about the plane crashes, there was
no need to talk to Mr. Bush or pull him away. The president didn't
leave immediately after receiving the news of the second crash from
Mr. Card because Mr. Bush's "instinct was not to frighten the
children by rushing out of the room," the spokesman added. [10]

—WALL STREET JOURNAL

Soul seer?

From his seat in the classroom, how did Bush know his staff was trying to get more facts and why didn't he know they would be so crappy at it? Twenty-five minutes later he walks to the podium to address the nation no less uninformed and ignorant.

Rooster boy:

Bush didn't have rush out of the room. He could strut like usual. Or do a cartwheel—who cares?

Dr. Spock:

Kids don't get scared when a person leaves a room unless the individual is on fire, singing "Copacabana" and juggling porcupine's.

Delegating war:

The staff isn't in charge. Ari and Andy don't decide if the Commander-in-Chief is needed when the country is under attack.

Useless political appendages:

No member of the staff was bright enough to call the FAA or the Defense Department. Many of them are later promoted to high ranking positions at FEMA.

And Weighs And Weighs

"I am a decisive person. I get the facts, weigh them thoughtfully and carefully, and decide." [11]

—GEORGE BUSH

Flash Forward 25 Minutes:

The president gathers the young props around him to tell them the country has been attacked.

9:05 am—Don't frighten kids.

9:30 am—Scare the apple juice out of them.

Mr. Sensitive

Anderson: Not Enough Facts To Upset Children
There's a four fact minimum—Bush Doctrine #5937

> *"But without all the facts at hand, George Bush had no intention*
> *of upsetting the schoolchildren who had come to read for him."* [12]

—CHRISTOPHER ANDERSEN "GEORGE & LAURA"

What's the standard?
Does the president need all of the facts before upsetting children, or just a majority of the facts?

Wanted by Interpol
BIN LADEN, Usama

Cinderella: 6-Year-Old Kid

Cinderella is an alias.
She knows what happens if you deviate from the White House talking points—you get outed as a short, flag burning, middle-schooler with close ties to Hugo Chavez.

Author: "Cinderella, do you know who the President of the United States is?"

Cinderella: "George Bush. He wears a tie and has white hair."

Author: "If President Bush was in your classroom to listen to you and your classmates read and said, "I'm sorry children, but there's something very important that I have do and I need to leave," would you be scared, Cinderella?"

Cinderella: "No."

Author: "Would you be mad?"

Cinderella: "No."

Author: "Would you be sad?"

Cinderella: "No."

Author: "Would you be worried?"

Cinderella: "Yes."

Author: "What would you be worried about?"

Cinderella: "I would be worried that he has something important to do."

Author: "You would be worried about the president?"

Cinderella: "Yes."

"I don't need people around me who are not steady...
And if there's kind of a hand-wringing attitude going on
when times are tough, I don't like it." [13]

—GEORGE BUSH

Dead Wood

Bush Not Needed
During The Attacks Says Press Secretary
President generally doesn't enter game until third quarter

> *"Given the fact that no one told the President's traveling party*
> *that additional aircraft had been hijacked, I don't know what*
> *difference it would have made had he left the room any earlier,*
> *other than perhaps to panic a frightened nation if his first reaction*
> *was suddenly to bolt from his chair and leave the room without any*
> *explanation. Under inconceivable pressure, Bush maintained his*
> *composure and sent an image of calm to the nation."* [14]

—ARI FLEISCHER "TAKING HEAT"

Radiating good vibes:
Bill Sammon says, "He [Bush] knew they were not transmitting images of
him in real time, since this event had not been set up for a live feed." [15]

Model of modesty:
George Bush is such a humble fellow—he actually refused to let anyone
boast about his magnificent "chair sitting" performance for several years.
The video wasn't put on White House Web site, or even allowed in political
TV ads—where the president chose to show bodies being removed from
Ground Zero, rather than brag about how he miraculously calmed the
nation on 9/11 without benefit of live television coverage.

Telepathic?
How did the Bush know that no one in the traveling party knew about
more hijackings? Did he suddenly become perceptive? Pretty spooky.

Vice versa?
Nobody told the president's traveling party that there **weren't** more
hijackings in progress.

Oracle of Sarasota:
Ari's right—it would have made no difference if the president had left the
classroom earlier. Even when Bush finally went to the holding room, he
didn't do anything to defend the country anyway.

Hello?

"Yes, hi…is this the FAA?
Good. Say, the President of the
United States wants to know what
the hell is going on? Yes. I'll hold.
[two seconds pass] What? An unknown number of hijacked planes
are still in the sky? Ok, thanks. have
a super nice day."

Overheard in NY:

"Oh Sid, it's awful hot in here,
what with the building being on
fire and all, but a chill just ran
down my spine. I just know the
president sprinted out of a room
with no explanation. He could pull a muscle and possibly cause an embarrassing lull in the conversation. I'm really frightened and panicked now."

Hypothetical History

In 640 B.C., the Spartan general
Kolja "Curly" Diakoumis sat down
on a big flat rock to project some
strength and calm as his regiment
was being overrun by a large band
of pissed off Messeneans. Survivors
of the battle found Curly's head,
with a serene expression on his face,
three days later at a flea market.

Barry Manilow:

Did the FAA put you on hold? Ask the Secret Service agents. Vice
President Cheney said, "the Secret Service has an arrangement with the
F.A.A. They had open lines after the World Trade Center was…"

—MEET THE PRESS, SEPTEMBER 16, 2001

Low IQ:

No bolting required, but nice try Ari. If Bush can't outwit a group of
second graders and leave a room without throwing the entire nation into
turmoil, he may need to tweak his social skills a hair?

He was mesmerizing:

Name two people who were watching Bush sit on TV, while the towers
burned. Write their names down and call the Secret Service immediately.

What a hassle, man:

Pressure? Oh, please. Try standing on a ledge with a 1000-foot drop on
one side and a fire on the other.

Pity:

Poor George. How could all those mean people expect him to do his job,
him being so delicate and all.

Time Bandit

Rove: President Left Classroom Within Moments
In less time than it takes to peruse some classified documents

> *"And the President was a little—you know, he didn't want to alarm the children. He knew the drill was coming to a close. So he waited for a few moments just too literally—not very long at all before he came to the close, and he came into the staff room which was literally located a short walk from the classroom. And he walked in."* [16]

> —KARL ROVE

Liar:
It was seven minutes.

The Patriot

President Allows Kids To Keep Reading
Interrupting children mid-sentence can trigger seizures—and acid reflux

> *"I will always admire the President's calm and self-control, allowing the kids to keep reading without his body or his words betraying the enormity of what he had just been told."* [17]

> —ARI FLEISCHER "TAKING HEAT"

Ready to rumble:
Tough guy and reigning crochet champ Karl Rove said, "I don't know about you, but moderation and restraint is not what I felt when I watched the twin towers crumble to the ground, a side of the Pentagon destroyed, and almost 3,000 of our fellow citizens perish in flames and rubble." [18]

Slim pickins:
Ari is pretty much forced to admire Bush for freezing up during a terrorist attack. What else is there?

> "Remember Jerry. It's not a lie, if you believe it."
>
> —GEORGE COSTANZA

Foursome!

In his book "Fighting Back," Bill Sammon, shoots for a Medal of Freedom with four rationalizations for the presidential paralysis in one paragraph…

Sammon I:
Curse The Liberal Media For Their Damnable Possible Future Misinterpretations

President Worried About The Press
And not the garlic press this time, which he would rather not talk about

> *"But there is no sense in rushing his exit. The press might interpret haste as distress."* [19]

—BILL SAMMON "FIGHTING BACK"

Phobic?
Fear of the press prevented Bush from acting? What a coincidence; fear of terrorists flying their plane into a building motivated the passengers on Flight 93 to fight their captors.

Sammon II:
Mr. Politically Correct

Bush Chooses Image Over Information
If anybody asks, it was a tough call

> *"Bush wondered whether he should excuse himself and retreat to the holding room, where he might be able to find out what was going on. But what kind of message would that send—the president abruptly getting up and walking out on a bunch of inner-city second graders at their moment in the national limelight."* [20]

—BILL SAMMON

Race relations expert:
Inner-city? Code for black kids. If they had been white, presumably the president could have left to do his job without sending any "message."

Cool anecdote though:
The kids now have a swell story for their grandchildren. The country was under attack, but the president just sat there like a moron. "I like thought he was like going to stroke out or something."

Hallmark moment:
The millionaire Bush, with the government checkbook, could have made it up to the kids later [still can]. Maybe fly them all on Air Force One to his ranch and spend a week with the youngsters. But don't touch the chainsaws, Johnny—those are important symbols of the presidents virility. The kids deserve something for being forced to sit there and watch him twitch.

He Read It Somewhere... Maybe On A Placemat

"I knew that if the nation's under attack, the role of the Commander-In-Chief is to respond forcefully to prevent other attacks from happening."

—GEORGE BUSH

❖ ❖ ❖

Sammon III: The Terrorists Would Win

Last Thing Nation Needed Was A Panicked President
Or more attacks—six of one and so forth—pretty much a wash

"Bush might look rattled, or worse, panicked. The last thing the nation needed at this moment was a panicked president. Such an image might even play into the hands of the attackers."[21]

—BILL SAMMON "FIGHTING BACK"

Well, I never!
Panic the nation by leaving a room?
How unrefined. What finishing
school did George go to, anyway?

Big bullies:
What the hell is Bill talking about?
What would the terrorists do—stop
the attacks and taunt the president for
freaking out? The younger murderers
can be so very cruel with their
teasing…

> ## No Actions Necessary At This Time
>
> *"I'll say it for the third time—
> the Constitution vests in the
> President as Commander in Chief
> the authority to take actions he
> deems necessary to protect and
> defend the United States."*
>
> —ARI FLEISCHER SEPTEMBER 13, 2001

> *Bush, Bush, sat on his tush*
> *When told of some killing*
> *He found it too thrilling*
> *And ran out of the room with a whoosh*

> *"Women—and I don't mean to limit that to the biological sense—*
> *always become hysterical at the first sign of trouble. They have no*
> *capacity to solve problems, so instead they fret."* [22]

—ANN COULTER

Sammon IV: Miss Congeniality

**Demeanor Almost As Important
As Actions, Senses President**
That's exactly what Ike told the boys before they hit the beaches at Normandy

> *"No, better to remain calm and sit tight for now. Bush sensed his*
> *demeanor would be almost as important as his actions in these first*
> *crucial moments. 'The real measure of a person is how he responds to*
> *bad news' he had written in his memoirs."* [23]

—BILL SAMMON

Omen:
It's true. We saw the real measure of the man.

Time toady:
First crucial moments? I'm afraid those passed the president by like he was sitting still. The hijackings started nearly an hour ago at 8:14 am.

No Demeanor Mentioned Here

We shall have the ability to respond rapidly and decisively to terrorism directed against us wherever it occurs, to protect Americans, arrest or defeat the perpetrators, respond with all appropriate instruments against the sponsoring organizations and governments and provide recovery relief to victims, as permitted by law.

—PRESIDENTIAL DIRECTIVE 39, 1995

❖ ❖ ❖

The Man Who Wasn't There

Chief Of Staff Explains Seven Minutes
It never happened

> *"I pulled away from the president, and not that many seconds later, the president excused himself from the classroom, and we gathered in the holding room and talked about the situation."* [24]

—ANDREW CARD

Body double:
The real George Bush left the room to do his job, while his stunt double, the guy who crashes the bikes and falls off Segways, sits in the classroom with a vacant look on his face.

Stopped watch:

It's "Card Time" again. If 420 seconds isn't that many, then Andrew Card isn't a liar. The seven minutes, the time that Bush and his staff members with time pieces find so admirable, is completely written off by the Chief of Staff. How dare he minimize Bush's noble contribution to the defense of our country? Who else would have taken the time to ponder what being under attack really truly meant before rashly trying to save lives? Who but George Bush would be talented enough to jump straight to the revenge stage without finishing the defense segment and flesh out the Bush Doctrine in his spare time? Seriously...who?

Vigorous Defense— Nothing About Facial Expression

It is the policy of the United States to deter, defeat and respond vigorously to all terrorist attacks on our territory and against our citizens, or facilities, whether they occur domestically, in international waters or airspace or on foreign territory.

—PRESIDENTIAL DIRECTIVE 39, 1995

Beat The Clock

President Leaves Classroom Shortly After 9:00 AM

Or, at 9:12 if you want to be picky

> "Andy approached the President, whispered into his ear, with the press before and the children before him, about the crash of the second plane. The President had been intending to make remarks about the first plane in that session, but he decided to wait until he could ascertain additional information, given the fact now that it was not one, but two, crashes, which was an immediate indication, of course, of the serious nature of this suggesting terrorism."

> "Then, as you know, the President returned to his hold, received additional information from Dr. Rice. Information was still very sketchy at that point—this is shortly after 9:00 a.m. And then the President proceeded—the decision was made by the President that he

would go and speak to the nation about what transpired. You have the record of that. And then the President immediately departed for the airport."

—ARI FLEISCHER SPEAKING TO THE PRESS ON 9/11

Time flies:
Fleischer magically wipes out 30 minutes.

Plot Wasn't Thick Enough

Bush Sat Idly
Still getting handle on people showing up without a proper invite—or money

"I would never sit idly if I had known what was coming on September 11! Had I known about the plot I would have used the whole force and fury of the United States to stop them." [25]

—GEORGE BUSH "THE LEADERSHIP GENIUS OF GEORGE W. BUSH"

Duh:
Even if he couldn't figure out the plot after the first attack, it was obvious after the second crash that plowing airliners into buildings was the plan, and yet the president still doesn't use force or fury. Fighter jets were summoned to protect his hide on Air Force One, but Bush didn't lift a finger to defend anyone else.

Fewer Minds Than You Think

"In the first few hours, I think the thing that was on everybody's mind was, how many more planes are coming?" [26]

—CONDI RICE

America Well Manicured Before GW

"Prior to September 11, all his [bin Laden] attacks had occurred during the era of Bill Clinton, who never responded forcefully. Indeed, American back then seemed averse to getting their fingernails dirty." [27]

—Bill Sammon

The Camera
Adds 7 Minutes To Everyone

Morris Understands
He's been there, man

> *"And I think that when Bush is criticized for those 7 minutes, those were on camera minutes. Listen, if 9/11 happened and Bush were in the Oval Office and he were alone and not on camera, and Card walked in and gave him a note and said another plane hit the towers, America's under attack, and he sat in his chair in the Oval Office staring into the distance for 7 minutes, get that man out of there. But on camera, under-reacting, not panicking, reassuring the country by his presence, by his stability, not causing mass panic—I really understand that." [28]*

—Dick Morris

What's a girl to do?
There's only one solution. Keep Bush locked up so he won't cause a national panic by leaving a room.

Out Of My Head
Hopelessly Devoted To Yoooou!

Coulter: Some People Too Picky About Defense
They get so melodramatic about every little attack on the country

> *"I would like liberals to explain to me what they think George Bush should have done—you know, run out of the classroom, rip open his shirt: Let the bullets hit me first! They're so childlike. For one thing, we didn't know what was going on. It was very public where the president was. The school has to be secured. You have to get Air Force One ready. Where are the terrorists? They're in air space, they're in the skies, all of this has to be secured, the school has to be secured. What's he going to do? Make a pay phone call? Call from his cell phone to Dick Cheney? He is the President of the United States, we don't need a presidential assassination in that 7 minutes. I'm quite sure the Secret Service wouldn't have let him run out and run around the school or do whatever liberals think he should be doing."* [29]

—ANN COULTER

✔ No running in the halls or outside. And, stay off the monkey bars—they're pretty sticky.

✔ No shirt tearing—wearing old "I Got Stoned With Thurgood Marshall" undershirt.

✔ No bullet taking; except for anonymous unimportant Secret Service guys or Clint Eastwood.

✔ Secure the school; be sure to lock doors so suicide planes can't get in.

✔ Get Air Force One gassed up—check the oil this time, Irv!

✔ Secure air space—call Air Force guys when we have time.

✔ No pay phones. Use the secure phones in the holding room unless you want to waste a ton of quarters like last time.

✔ No cell phones—we sure don't want this circus showing up on tape.

✔ Call Cheney (screw Rumsfeld—what an asshole).

✔ No getting assassinated, no matter how glamorous it sounds at the moment.

Civil Servant

President's Job Is
Not To Run Fire Department Explains Morris
He always gets everyone wet, anyway—or killed

> *"And when we criticize George Bush, we are really asking him to be superhuman. When you're confronted with something like that, in the first few minutes, you just watch and absorb it. And let's also understand that he's the President of the United States. He's not an emergency worker. His job is not to run the fire department or the police department. His job is to be president."* [30]

—DICK MORRIS

Dick's right:
I mean a suck-up.

Kicked upstairs:
The military—Bush gets to run that, though, right?

All Puckered Up
And Ready For Duty, Sir!

King: President Waiting For Staff
To Find Out What Happened
Evidently, the congressman has never met Bush's staff

"There was nothing he could have done at that moment. He was waiting for his staff to find out what happened. Once that was done, he got up and calmly walked out. On all accounts he was on the phone immediately with the vice president, with Condoleeza Rice, with cabinet officials, directing what had to be done, in full command." [31]

—PETER KING

Weak stomach:
Nothing could be done—that's the spirit. Rockets red glare, indeed.

Loose Lips

If Bush Talks, More Attacks Are Launched
Or if he goes under 50 mph in a bus

"Bush was probably sitting there saying to himself, I don't want to say anything that makes more of these attacks possible." [32]

—DICK MORRIS

Probably:
That's not what Bush said he was thinking, but if Dick wants to call him a liar—it's a good possibility.

9:12 AM

The Commander-in-Chief leaves the classroom and enters the holding room at the Booker Elementary School.

Review

9:05-9:12 AM

At 9:03 am, United Airlines Flight 175 crashes into the South Tower of the World Trade Center on live television.

At 9:05 am, the Chief of Staff decides telling the president about an ongoing attack on the country is the right thing to do. It took him two minutes to figure that one out.

Reasons Commander-in-Chief stays in classroom for another 7 minutes:

1. Bush didn't want to scare the kids.
2. Bush needed to project strength and calm.
3. Bush was avoiding assassination.
4. Bush was waiting for more information.
5. Bush was waiting until he could better understand what was going on.
6. Bush wasn't needed.
7. Bush didn't want to frighten the nation.
8. Bush didn't want to play into the hands of the terrorists.
9. Bush didn't want to give the media the wrong impression.
10. Bush thought more attacks would be triggered if he moved.
11. Bush felt that his demeanor was more important than taking action.
12. Bush didn't know of the other hijackings.
13. Bush knew he needed to do something, but didn't know what it was.
14. Bush needed to ponder the 50's and 60's when the only fear was nuclear annihilation.
15. Bush didn't want to offend black people.
16. Bush needed to ponder the meaning of being under attack.
17. Bush needed to plan revenge and develop the Bush doctrine.
18. Bush was stunned.
19. Bush didn't want to panic the nation.
20. Bush was absorbing the information.
21. Bush wasn't allowed to run around.
22. Bush was waiting for the school to be secured.
23. Bush was waiting for Air force One to be readied.

However, Andy Card said Bush actually left the room within seconds and Karl Rove maintained that Bush literally left the room within moments. They lied.

Meanwhile, during the 7 minutes of presidential immobility...

Vice President Cheney meets with his staff. They talk about getting a task force together and also start to figure out what to do.

Condi Rice adjourns a staff meeting and convenes with Cheney.

Donald Rumsfeld, aka the Secretary of Defense, continues with an intelligence briefing.

An unknown number of hijacked commercial airliners are in the air.

The Air Force has scrambled jets to intercept hijacked planes, yet no order has been given from the president to shoot down suicide airliners before they reach populated areas. Bush maintains he was not told about and was unable to find out about other hijacked planes until some point after his 9:30 am television statement.

Thousands of New Yorker's rush to the World Trade Center to assist with the rescue operations. Some Trade Center occupants are trapped above the fire and others find escape routes blocked. Some people caught between fire and great heights opt to jump.

Fearing more attacks, New York officials start evacuating landmark buildings and other possible terrorist targets like bridges and tunnels. People in Washington D.C. buildings, including the White House and Pentagon are not evacuated.

CHAPTER FIVE

Taking Care Of Business

9:12–9:30 AM
18 Minutes

"...I would calmly stand up and thank the teacher and thank the children and go take care of business."
—GEORGE BUSH TO LARRY KING

"The focus was on the President's statement to the nation. The only decision made during this time was to return to D.C."
—9/11 COMMISSION REPORT

"Can't anybody here play this game?"
—CASEY STENGEL

At 9:12 am, President Bush left the classroom and entered the holding room set up with secure communications for his visit. Not knowing what to do, he calls the Vice President, as is the custom. Throughout American history, the VP has been called upon by the president to give guidance during emergencies—Washington, Lincoln, the Roosevelt's and Polk all depended on their Vice President to call the shots. Even Grover Cleveland relied on "old what's his name" for instructions on many nonconsecutive occasions.

Bad news this time, though—because he's spent more time meeting with Enron than working on his terrorism assignment, Cheney doesn't have a clue, either. So instead of doing something to stop the terrorists from killing Americans, they begin to discuss the wording for a speech Bush intends to read to the country at 9:30 am—a time determined before the day even started. Have to stay on schedule—got to be crisp, you know.

When the president told Larry King he went to "take care of business," he didn't say his idea of "business" was to spend the next 18 minutes writing a statement in the middle of a terrorist attack.

9:12 AM

Daddy Day Care

Bush: "We're At War"—Get Me Cheney
And a grape snow cone—with a little umbrella deal

> *"And he came in sort of between me and the television and looked at the television as the second plane—they had replayed the footage of the second plane flying in. And he said in a very firm—you know, it was sort of quiet, his voice, but it was very firm and very solid, and you could hear the steel in it. He said, 'We're at war. Give me the Vice President. Get me the director of the FBI,' and tried to get people on the telephone."* [1]

—KARL ROVE MSNBC INTERVIEW 9/11/2002

Non sequitur:
The house is on fire—get me my barber!

Brass ass:
Steely? In lieu of real leadership, a metal like tone of voice will have to do. The president didn't do anything to protect the country, so Karl is left with describing voice patterns.

> *"My time in the Guard taught me the importance of a well-trained and well-equipped military. It gave me respect for the chain of command."* [2]
>
> —GEORGE BUSH "A CHARGE TO KEEP"

Based On A Good Imagination

In the movie "DC 9/11" Bush calls Rumsfeld from the holding room, ordering the Secretary to put the military on high alert. He also tells Rummy to "get your boys up there." In real life, none of that happened, but even though Bush and staff members were interviewed prior to filming, the fantasy version makes it to the screen. If Bush is so proud of his actual actions, why did film need to be enhanced with lies?

Rove Colored Glasses

Vice President Not Available For Call Says Rove
Taking a bubble bath—and yes, alone this time

> *"We got the director of the FBI, but the Vice President, we didn't get because at this moment, the Vice President was being moved literally, grabbed by his belt, lifted off the floor and grabbed by a Secret Service agent and moved to the bunker because the plane was approaching the White House."* [3]

—Karl Rove MSNBC Interview 9/11/2002

Lie:
In fact, according to "everyone" else, the vice president talked to the president. Cheney wasn't evacuated from his White House office until 9:36 am, about 20 minutes later. By then, Bush was in the limo, making a break for the airport. The dough boy Rove lies and pushes the time forward to cover for the president's lollygagging at the school.

Attacks Over...
Bush Works On Acceptance Speech For Prestigious "Heckava Job" Award

President Calls Cheney
Vice President orders Bush to project steadfastness instead of calm— president arches left eyebrow

> *"Mr. Bush walked into a classroom set up with a secure phone. He called the vice president, pulling the phone cord tight as he spun to see the attack on TV. Then he grabbed a legal pad and quickly wrote his first words to the nation."* [4]

—60 Minutes II

Like ragweed:
They grow up so fast. It seems like only a few years ago that Dick Cheney was doing business with terrorist sponsoring nations, and now he's advising the president during a terrorist attack.

Chain gang:
Cheney is not in the chain of command, but Secretary of Defense Rumsfeld is very busy writing up some new witty rejoinders and can't be disturbed.

Mighty pen:
We're under attack! Does anybody have a pen and paper? This situation calls for a speech and a stern letter to the editor.

Although He May Ask How

"George W. Bush will never seek a permission slip to defend the American people."

Red alert:
Junior is taking care of business again. Inform the SEC and watch your wallet.

—DICK CHENEY
2004 REPUBLICAN CONVENTION

Great Scott:
He's multitasking! If only the president had one of those Internets handy.

9:17 AM

The Federal Aviation Administration shuts down all New York City area airports.[5]

No Meetings or Speeches in NYC
ABC reports that New York is now implementing a procedure called the Archangel Operation. It involves a lockdown of the city, and the evacuation of buildings considered to be potential terrorist targets. New York officials are not assuming the attacks are over.

Who Moved My Cheesecake

Cheney And Rice Meet
To Discuss Mobilizing Task Force

Meetings scheduled to tackle pre-discussion issues and coordinate
the agenda

> *"Bush talked first with the vice president. He was already huddling*
> *with Rice to talk about mobilizing an anti-terrorism task force."* [6]

—BILL SAMMON FIGHTING BACK

Corporate defense:
Let's have a meeting, think outside the box and talk about new paradigms.
Order some tasty sandwiches—we're going to be here for awhile.

No juice:
Cheney can try to mobilize
anything he wants, but he's still
only the vice president.

Minutemen:
Paul Revere was faster on horseback
than these rubes.

ABC Live

John Miller: "What we were
talking about is, there's been
a great frustration since the
bombing of the World Trade
Center, which the suspects later
told federal authorities were
intended to take the building
down, that it didn't have a larger
effect. And US intelligence, FBI
people, for years have heard that
they've always wanted to try and
finish that job off, to take the
buildings out, and it was another
viable target."

9:21 AM

The Port Authority orders all bridges and tunnels in the New York area closed in anticipation of more attacks.[7]

Unaware it was Flight 11 that hit the North Tower; the FAA tells NEADS that Flight 11 is still airborne and heading for Washington, D.C.

New York is evacuating possible terrorist targets, but people in the White House and Pentagon aren't moved.

The president prepares for his TV appearance. He smears his lipstick while drinking a Snapple and has to reapply—dang it.

Still—no actions are taken by Bush or the Defense Secretary to defend the country.

❖ ❖ ❖

Let There Be Talking

President Needed To Make A Statement
The first of 4,979 September 11 speeches in the 2004 election cycle.

> *"And the President said, 'I need to make a statement.'*
> *So he went into the classroom where he was supposed to make*
> *remarks on education and made his first remarks."* [8]

—Karl Rove

Oh Karl, you scamp:
Bush started writing notes for his TV appearance as soon as he went to the holding room at 9:12 am. He didn't just make the decision and walk directly to the podium. That would be silly. It takes at least 15 minutes to find the right words to tell people what they already know. The president didn't go to the microphones until 9:30 am.

9:23 AM

Fighter jets are scrambled from Langley Air Force Base.

Bush is still working on statement. Four score and…d'oh!

American Airlines Flight 77 is now headed east towards Washington, D.C.

In New York, survivors of the initial impacts on the towers struggle
to stay alive.

9:25 AM

A nationwide ground stop of all air traffic is ordered by the FAA.

But Nothing Too Frilly

Special Place Needed To Make Decisions
And not on the toilet this time

> *"First of all, we had to figure out what we were going to do and
> where we were going to make decisions from. And the Secret Service
> and Mil Aide was in the process of getting information about where
> the president ought to go. One thing for certain, I needed to get out of
> where I was."* [9]

—GEORGE BUSH

Molasses:
It's been 30 minutes since the first attack and the president's **"first"** move
is to decide where to make decisions? Oh, boy—better call Dick again.

Persnickety:
What's wrong with making decisions at the school? It's already set up with
secure communications. Grab some pine, dude.

Pet rock:
Is anybody claiming this guy as a dependent? Mr. Decisive Leader even needs help deciding where to be.

Funhouse mirror:
Bush needs a special place to decide where to decide where to decide where to decide…

Bail like a snail:

"I choose George W. Bush because he is a leader we can depend on to make the tough decisions and the right decisions."

—GENERAL TOMMY FRANKS,
2004 REPUBLICAN CONVENTION

As the Commander-in-Chief fiddles with the roadmap, people are dying in the towers and hijacked planes are on a path towards Washington, D.C.

The Reflex Time
Of A Three Toed Sloth

**Bush: Response Mechanism
Sharp And Ready To Go**
Doesn't understand meaning of response, mechanism, sharp or ready

> *"I didn't spend that much time about my own safety because I knew others were worried about that. What I was interested in is making sure that the response mechanism that was under my control was sharp and ready to go. And that meant defense, for starters."* [10]

—GEORGE BUSH

Carried away:
Defense? So soon? Let's not be hasty, George. So far, there have only been two attacks. Just because some nut cases think the government should always be on defense doesn't make it true. Slow down, or people will expect you to protect them all of the time—and that would be a pain.

Shirk jerk:
Psych. Bush decided to run away
first and worry about defense later.

*"The terrorists misunderestimated
America and its leader."*[11]

—THE LEADERSHIP GENIUS
OF GEORGE W. BUSH

Flight 77 is 12 minutes away from the Pentagon.

In New York, thousands of rescue workers and regular citizens face the
danger head-on to help others—Bush figures Florida is too close for comfort.

Holmes & Watson Together Again

Bush & Cheney:
Terrorists Probably Behind Attacks
Duo also cracks mystery of president's high name recognition in 1999

*"He and Cheney agreed that terrorists were probably behind
the attacks, and the president decided to say so to the nation."*[12]

—BILL SAMMON

J'accuse:
Instead of fighting the terrorists, Bush would boldly point the finger at
them and then slap the brutes with his mittens.

Call 867-5309

President Seeks Information
Keeps forgetting to dial nine—talks to cafeteria lady 17 times

> *"He and Andy worked the two phones in the hold, seeking what little information was available."* [13]

—ARI FLEISCHER

Torture somebody already!
With the entire U.S. government at his disposal, the leader of the free world, a decorated phone dialer and renowned bossy pants, couldn't find out about the other hijacked planes. Ever since Bush talked to Condi Rice at 8:55 am, he and his staff have been trying to get information. He heads to the podium at 9:30 am still oblivious. Wire tap the FAA, maybe?

Sorry...not safe:
Luckily for the terrorists, one of the few government officials to presume the attacks were finished happened to be the president—the only person in the world with the authority to order the Air Force to shoot down a commercial airliner.

The Words
Flowed Like Delicious Oil

President And VP
Discuss Messaging For Statement
Slip in no-bid contract for Halliburton to pave Alaska with crushed antlers

> *"We discussed a statement that he (Bush) might make, and the first statement he made describing this as an act of apparent terrorism flowed out of those conversations. While I was there, over the next several minutes, watching developments on the television and as we started to get organized to figure out what to do, my Secret Service agents came in and, under these circumstances, they just move. They don't say "sir" or ask politely. They came in and said, 'Sir, we have to leave immediately,' and grabbed me and...* [14]

—DICK CHENEY

File this under imbeciles:
Started to get organized? Grab me some of the color coded folders, will you—and three bear claws? Goddamnit—who took my stapler?

Cementheads:
Maybe this is how things were handled at Harken, but when the country is under attack, there isn't time for "discussing a statement" or dumping stock.

Live: Bush gets scooped
CNN reports that a U.S. official has declared the two airplane crashes at the World Trade Center to be acts of terrorism. They also note that President Bush will be coming out shortly to give a statement.

9:28 AM

United Airlines Flight 93 is hijacked.

President Bush takes a deep breath and puts on his "somewhat concerned and puzzled" face for the cameras. Stuffs sock down pants for good luck.

9:30 AM

That's A Wrap

Bush: Attacks Over—
Will Hunt Down Folks Responsible
Pentagon hit eight minutes later—talking points updated for Armstrong Williams

"Ladies and gentlemen, this is a difficult moment for America. I, unfortunately, will be going back to Washington after my remarks. Secretary Rod Paige and the Lt. Governor will take the podium and discuss education. I do want to thank the folks here at Booker Elementary School for their hospitality. Today we've had a national tragedy. Two airplanes have crashed into the World Trade Center in an apparent terrorist

attack on our country. I have spoken to the Vice President, to the Governor of New York, to the Director of the FBI, and have ordered that the full resources of the federal government go to help the victims and their families, and to conduct a full-scale investigation to hunt down and to find those folks who committed this act. Terrorism against our nation will not stand. And now if you would join me in a moment of silence. May God bless the victims, their families, and America. Thank you very much."[15]

—GEORGE BUSH, EXPLAINING EVENTS TO TELEVISION VIEWERS

Less is less:
That's it? "Find those folks." A well spent 18 minutes, indeed.

Statuette of freedom:
And the award for best "Master of Ceremonies during an ongoing terrorist attack" goes to the artist formerly know as "Jeb's not too bright older brother"— George W. Bush! Woo hoo!

Premature withdrawal:
GW would later have same problem with Iraq; nothing seems to end on cue.

Oh, and by the way:
If you live in Washington, D.C...

ABC Live
Peter Jennings: "President clearly shaken, I think, one can say, confirming what we think we all knew, which was that two aircraft in an act of terrorism crashed into the twin trade towers."

Stupid Is As Stupid Does

Bush Unaware Of Hijacked Planes
FAA not on "friends and family" calling plan

> *As he spoke, Mr. Bush didn't know that two more hijacked jets were streaking toward Washington.* [16]

—60 MINUTES II

Loopless:
Of course Bush didn't know what's going on—how would the Most Powerful Man on Earth possibly get information from government agencies under his command?

The Post Speech Self Analysis

> *"I'm also not very analytical. You know I don't spend a lot of time thinking about myself, about why I do things."*

—GEORGE BUSH

The president is very proud of himself, believing even years later, that his 9/11 duties had been fulfilled by delivering a speech in the middle of a terrorist attack without passing out.

American Idle

"I Knew People Were Watching," Says President
Nothing else was on

> *"I remember I had to convince myself to be as calm and resolute as possible, because I knew people were watching."* [17]

—GEORGE BUSH

What a dick:
New Yorkers and passengers on the hijacked planes are just trying to survive—quit preening, scrape off the rouge and do your job.

Mission Accomplished: Bush Delivers Speech Without Drooling

President Needed To Send Sense Of Calm
Tries out the untested "quivering and perspiring" technique

> *"I can be an emotional guy. And I was worried, emotional, about loss of life, because the magnitude of what happened had come home. At the same time, I knew I needed to send a sense of, you know, calm in the face of what could be panic. And I think I was able to achieve that. I can't remember having to be conscious, conscious of how—It's the first time I've really—Usually when I get up at these things, at these big events, I just kind of let 'er go and hope for the best. This moment, I was conscious of what was going to happen, because I was feeling emotions inside of me. I was not doubtful. I was firm in what I knew we needed to do."* [18]

> —GEORGE BUSH

True humanitarian:
Bush is worried about the loss of life, but he's not quite ready to do anything about it. Of course, it's really the thought that counts.

Firm & humble:
Bush will boast about pretty much anything.

Slow leak:
NOW, the magnitude of the crisis is starting to seep in—45 minutes after the first attack?

Dunce:
If Bush thought that giving a televised statement was the proper response to a terrorist attack, we're better off if he just stays on vacation.

Malingerer:
Why wait until 9:30 am? Bush would have given the very important statement earlier, but word has it he was waiting for the "Fighting Terrorism Resolutely With Hardly Any Crying 2001" backdrop to arrive. Unfortunately, he had to start without it. And Karl wanted to have the Corp of Engineers turn the school slightly, so the sun would shine through a window lightly on the president's face as he spoke—but the idea was ruled out after two caucuses and a 15-minute meeting in the tiny elementary school cloakroom.

"What you saw was my gut reaction coming out."

—GEORGE BUSH

Later, when Bush and Karen Hughes realize the stupidity of writing a speech during a terrorist attack, they try to minimize or erase the wasted time. Sammon and Fleischer didn't get the memo.

Didn't Waste Time Writing Statement

No Word Massaging Says Bush
Just a quick rub down

"I don't know why... I'll tell you this, we didn't sit around massaging the words. I got up there and just spoke. What you saw was my gut reaction coming out"[19]

—GEORGE BUSH

Wasted Time Writing Statement

Sharpie Used To Write Statement
Bic rejected as too delicate for masculine task

> *"Fleischer and Bartlett hastily drafted a statement, but Bush wanted to change and put it into his own words. Using his Sharpie, he scribbled 3 pages of notes on crinkly white paper. He gathered them up, got to his feet, and headed for the library."* [20]

—BILL SAMMON

Didn't Waste Time Writing Statement

Bush Speaks Without Script
Manliness rating jumps three points

> *"The president didn't want anything written out, Dan [Bartlett] reported: 'He'll just say something quick so we can leave.'"* [21]

—KAREN HUGHES

Wasted Time Writing Statement

Bush Writes Remarks On Note Cards
Specially embossed "Attack 2001"

> *"In longhand on five-by-eight note cards, the President wrote the remarks he would deliver to the crowd that awaited his arrival in the auditorium."* [22]

—ARI FLEISCHER

Holding Room Review
9:12–9:30 AM
18 Brain Dead Minutes

The president made calls to Cheney, FBI Director Mueller, Governor Pataki and Rice. By all accounts, they were nice visits.

An unknown number of skyjacked planes are still in the air, including Flight 77, which is bearing down on Washington, D.C.

Bush assumed the attacks were over and wasted time fussing over a statement for a 9:30 am television appearance. Less naïve, New York officials evacuate landmark buildings, and close bridges and tunnels in anticipation of further attacks.

He's the president, but Bush couldn't get information about the other presumed hijacked planes.

Cheney said that the Secret Service had an open line to the FAA, but for some reason, none of the agents mentioned the other planes to the president or anyone else in the traveling party—and evidently no one asks.

People in the Pentagon, White House and other D.C. buildings sit at their desks unaware a suicide plane is headed their way. The vice president is evacuated to a bunker, though. His life is valuable.

Defense Secretary Rumsfeld is too busy to get involved with some piddly terrorist attack. He went on with his regular schedule. He would later say that it wasn't his problem.

Flight 93 is hijacked.

A counterterrorism taskforce may have been formed.

Bush and Cheney put their heads together to find the right words to explain what everyone can see with their own eyes.

President Bush speaks to the television cameras and is very proud of his performance.

Thousands of people in New York are fighting for their lives.

No decisions were made during the president's time in the holding room
at the school except to leave Sarasota. Eighteen minutes have disappeared—
Rosemary Woods would have been proud.

CHAPTER SIX

The Great
Foggy Escape

9:30–10:03 AM
33 Minutes From Goodbye To Up In The Sky

"I think war is a dangerous place."
—GEORGE BUSH MAY 7, 2003

After Bush's tremendously superfluous TV appearance at 9:30 am, another 15 minutes pass before his motorcade reaches Air Force One and it is almost 10 am before the plane takes off. The president is having a lot of phone conversations and secure phones were at the school, in the limo and on the plane, but he still doesn't order any defensive action.

From Bush's speech at 9:30 am until the crash of Flight 93 in a Pennsylvania field at 10:03 am, the president does nothing to protect the people. No military, no evacuations—nothing. As the attacks come to a close, the tally of Bush actions during the entire crisis is easy to cipher. The total is zero.

His favorite excuse? Fog.

9:30 AM

President Bush appears on TV to tell the nation of an apparent terrorist attack. Everyone is on board with that assessment.

9:33 AM

There Was a Hotline?
Reagan National Airport picks up a hotline to the Secret Service to warn that an uncommunicative aircraft is headed towards Washington, D.C. [1]

—9/11 COMMISSION REPORT

9:35 AM

The president's motorcade departs the Booker school and heads for Air Force One.

Leave All Children Behind

President Works The Phones Again
Sells three subscriptions to Better Homes & Gardens

> *"Bush worked the phones as the limo careened left onto University Parkway."* [2]

—BILL SAMMON FIGHTING BACK

Teen line:
Is he talking to Dick AGAIN?

Put Mommy dearest on hold:
How about evacuating the Pentagon, White House and other Washington landmark buildings? Cheney isn't the only person in the city worth saving.

Attitude adjustment:
Enough calm already—the pilots in the F-16's are waiting for orders.

Snubbed?
Why won't anyone give poor George the facts? The Secret Service has been told about a plane heading towards the Capitol—they have the facts. The FAA has the facts. The military knows what's going on, except for Rumsfeld. Break out the hoods, German Shepherds and 12-volt batteries and demand some respect.

9:36 AM

Langley AFB fighter jets are ordered to run to the White House.

Secret Service agents take Vice President Cheney from his White House office to a secure bunker. Most White House employees are left to fend for themselves.

Flight 93 reverses course and heads east.

There is still no evacuation or movement to more secure locations for people at the Pentagon.

❖ ❖ ❖

Only 963 Miles From The Front

Bush Blinded By Fog
Turned out to be smudge pots—and some slimy rovelike gunk on the windshield

> *"There is a fog of war. At this point, the information was sketchy, and the facts were just flying at us."* [3]

—GEORGE BUSH

How ironic:
Bush doesn't have enough facts to make any decisions, but the facts are just flying at him. Nobody told us, can't get any information, there was too much information, gotta have all the facts—oh well, the attacks are over. Go for a bike ride or something.

Wag The Fog

Fog Of War On The Phone Too
It's almost exactly like being in combat—except for the explosions and tacky off-the-rack clothing

> *"Well, the President was on the phone, and there was a fog of war. I mean, I've turned to people who have been in combat talk about the fog of war, and it really does exist. It was not real clarity as to what was going on. The President knew we had been attacked. The question is by whom and what other attacks were underway."* [4]

—KARL ROVE

Complete bullshit:
But what else can be expected from the Bullshit Artist's mentor?

Clarity:
As we all know, the president can't function without clarity. And, no one is allowed to talk about the president without using the word clarity. And he used have a hamster named Clarity. We get it, OK?

Nonviolent mood swing:
Now Bush is concerned about other attacks? A few minutes ago he was giving the "post assault" speech.

Irrelevant at this moment:
Who is attacking us? Who cares?—kill them.

Smokescreen

The Fog Was Indescribable
But let me tell you about it for ten minutes

> *"Remember there were reports that the State Department had been hit by a bomb. We received reports that there was a plane circling over Kentucky. The plane, Flight 93, was thought to be heading to*

Camp David. There was a report that there were planes or objects en route to Crawford. I really became—you know, you really know that in a moment like that, you know, you sort of see people as they really are, but you also see that steadiness becomes important because it really is—there is a fog of war. There is a, you know—" [5]

—KARL ROVE

Gibberish:

Could this explain why Turd Blossom and the walking speech impediment get along so well?

Immaterial nothingness:

That's a good idea; let's all just remember the reports of things that **didn't happen** and leave it at that.

Stand back and pretend to supervise:

Bush doesn't have to deal with each report personally, thank goodness— he's barely qualified to mow the South Lawn, but we have people for that stuff—a military. Quit bitching about the fog, pick up the phone and order the armed forces to defend the country.

Modus Operandi

Rice Knew It Was Al Qaida

Although, no one could have imagined this type of attack

"It was not very long before I think anyone who knew the MO of al Qaida had exactly the thought, this is al Qaida. It smelled like al Qaida. It felt like al Qaida, the kind of grandiose character of it, the attention-getting character of it. I think we knew pretty early on, and of course a little bit later on in the day, George Tenet, the CIA director, confirmed that the CIA's assessment was that it was al Qaida. But standing in the bunker only a few minutes after I had gotten there, I was pretty clear, in my own mind, that it was al Qaida." [6]

—CONDI RICE

Predictable:

Well, I'll be darned. It flew like a duck. It exploded like a duck. I guess the attacks were imaginable.

9:37:46 AM

Pentagon Hit By American Airlines Flight 77

What? Huh? I Was Awake!

Rumsfeld Had No Idea What Hit Pentagon
Unfolding trend too subtle for Princeton grad—"What am I, psychic?"

> *"A bomb? I had no idea. I looked out the window and raced down the corridors till the smoke was too bad and then went outside, and saw the devastation and talked to an eyewitness who told me that he had seen an aircraft plow into the Pentagon between the first and second floor."* [7]

> —Donald Rumsfeld

A Moron? Perhaps not:
Moments before Flight 77 hit the Pentagon, Rumsfeld said, "Believe me, this isn't over yet. There's going to be another attack, and it could be us." [8]

But then again, probably yes:
Why doesn't the great wit get his people out of the way? It's the VERY least he could do. Hundreds of dead and wounded—needlessly.

Walk-About Down By The Billabong

Plane Strikes Pentagon
Rumsfeld goes to crash site—leaves what's-his-name, the tall dude with the hat in charge

"I went outside to determine what had happened. I was not there long, apparently, because I am told I was back in the Pentagon, with a crisis action team, by shortly before or after 10:00 am."

—DONALD RUMSFELD TO 9/11 COMMISSION

My Heavens:
The Pentagon has been hit, too. Such a surprise—and only 36 minutes after the second attack on the World Trade Center.

AWOL:
Don didn't leave his post for too long—only about the time it takes an airliner to travel 200 miles.

No moral compass:
The Defense Secretary is wandering around with no watch, no cell phone, no pager—luckily he wasn't picked up by a couple of guys in white smocks looking for strays.

Still the man:
At this writing, Rumsfeld is still the Secretary of Defense.

Man The Desks

Rumsfeld Declares
Pentagon Victims Casualties Of War
Covers all asses nicely on the "left people in their offices to die" issue

"The president, of course, has made clear that the attacks were not just acts of terror. They were acts of war, military strikes against the United States of America. As such, those Department of Defense employees who were injured or killed were not just victims of terror. They were combat casualties, brave men and women who risked their lives to safeguard our freedom. And they paid for our liberty with their lives." [9]

—DONALD RUMSFELD DoD NEWS BRIEFING SEPTEMBER 27, 2001

Combat casualties:
Yes. But, they didn't need to be.

9:40 AM

The FAA stops all flight operations at U.S. airports.

9:45 AM

Bush's motorcade arrives at the airport and he boards Air Force One—
he orders a Vanilla Diet Coke and a tuna sandwich with extra net.

Stop The Music!

Cheney Ordered To Brief Congressional Leaders
But be brief

> *"The president got on the phone with Cheney, whom he had nick-
> named "Vice," and instructed him to brief congressional leaders."* [10]

—Bill Sammon

Backburner:
Brief Congressmen? About what—all the fog? Somebody please brief
the president. Bush is the only person who can order the shoot-down of
a commercial airliner and he doesn't know it.

Wiener nickname:
But still better than "fat bastard."

Unforeseeable:
The jackals on Flight 93 ignore
the time-out for briefings and
continue with their plan to crash
the airliner into a Washington,
D.C. landmark building—in clear
violation of the "Bush Conventions
of two minutes ago."

At the battle of Bladensburg in
August 1814, President James
Madison arrived on horseback
with a borrowed pair of dueling
pistols. Everything went to hell
shortly thereafter, as the British
overran American forces and went
on to Washington, D.C. and burned
much of it to the ground—but at
least the leader of our country
made a showing.

9:46 AM

Lost
Staffers are trying to locate Rumsfeld and General Myers.

—9/11 Commission Report

That's Odd
"First, the rules of engagement ought to be thought of in this way, that Americans can have a high degree of certainty, it seems to me: the president, the Secretary of Defense and the combatant commanders are never more than a minute or two away from a secure phone." [11]

—Donald Rumsfeld DoD News Briefing September 27, 2001

❖ ❖ ❖

Run Forrest, Run!

Bush Made No Major Decisions
Until Reaching Air Force One
President can't think clearly unless at least 800 miles from danger, very high—and at a lofty altitude

> *In the Dec. 4, 2001, town-hall meeting, the President said he didn't begin to make major decisions about the emergency until he was back aboard his plane. "I got on the phone from Air Force One, asking to find out the facts," he said.* [12]

—Wall Street Journal March 22, 2004

Hello?
Is this the facts department? I'll have two facts, please. What? Yes, to go, please. I don't need ketchup.

Busy signal?
The president still didn't give the order to defend the country from suicide planes until 30 minutes after getting on Air Force One.

Give Me Liberty Or Give Me A Fast Boeing 747-200B Jet With Cushy Couches And A Waffle Bar

Bush Unclear On Duties

Thinks he gets paid for making asinine remarks—and running away like a fluffy little bunny

> *"'We're at war.' That's what we're paid for, boys. We are going to take care of this. When we find out who did this, they are not going to like me as president. Somebody is going to pay."* [13]

—GEORGE BUSH

How do you like me now?

Bin Laden looked pretty happy about how things worked out—almost giddy.

Redundancy:

Bush keeps telling people we're at war. What is he, the narrator? Join the war already and shut up with the voiceovers.

Way overpaid:

The taxpayers get screwed again. Just wait…it doesn't get any better.

Too Bad We Were Attacked By Terrorists Instead Of History

"On September 11th al Qaeda attacked again. But this time they made a terrible mistake. There's one thing they didn't bank on. They didn't bank on George W. Bush. He didn't run from history. He faced it."

—GOVERNOR GEORGE PATAKI
2004 REPUBLICAN CONVENTION,
EXPLAINING HOW AL QAEDA
MADE A TERRIBLE MISTAKE
BY SUCCEEDING WITH THEIR PLAN
ON GEORGE W. BUSH'S WATCH.

Cut And Run

Men Of Action Needed
Author confuses moment of maximum peril with an eternity of shameful reflection

> *"At this moment of maximum peril, the president needed men of action."* [14]

—BILL SAMMON

Maximum baloney:
We needed a president of action, but it's too late now—Bush blew his chance to be a hero a long time ago.

Also Needed:
People who can keep their balance on a getaway plane.

> *"...cowards cut and run, Marines never do."*

—REP. JEAN SCHMIDT,
QUOTING CONSTITUENT ON THE
FLOOR OF CONGRESS

9:57 AM

On Flight 93—
People In Real Danger
And Not Retreating
...the passenger assault began. Several passengers had terminated phone calls with loved ones in order to join the revolt. One of the callers ended her message as follows: "Everyone's running up to first class. I've got to go. Bye."

—9/11 COMMISSION REPORT

Luckily for Washington, D.C. and the United States, Bush wasn't on Flight 93. He might have projected strength and calm, and then wrote a statement to announce the aircraft had been hijacked—probably by terrorist hijackers.

9:59 AM

The South Tower of the World Trade Center collapses.

10:00 AM

Strategery

Still Too Foggy To Do Anything Says Bush
And my juice box straw poked me in the left eyeball—really hard!

> *"There is a fog of war. You have heard about it, and you have read about it. Well, there is one. We had all kinds of reports. Once I was able to focus on what the conditions were in the country, I was able to think more clearly think about what we needed to do. The first thing we had to do was make sure we understood what the heck was going on."* [15]

—GEORGE BUSH

Baloney:
A president doesn't need every detail to act. Based on the comments of our new authority on fog—a person would get the sense that the United States had only one fighter jet, two helicopters and bass boat—and Bush had to personally figure out where to send each one.

Comprehension clog:
What's to understand? The country is under attack—turn the military loose to defend the American people. Then you can hide.

Lame excuse:
Once he was able to focus? All he's been doing for the last hour is contemplating, navel gazing and writing notes. The people on Flight 93 were able to act without an hour of reflection and self-pity. Thousands in New York and Washington, D.C. ran to the scene of the disasters without delay, Tom Delay or Ken Lay. Very weak.

Bottom line:
After the attacks were over and everything calmed down, the president was able to hone in on the problem and close the barn door.

Just Sweep It Under...

President Speaks To Rumsfeld
74 Minutes After First Attack
Made calls alphabetically

> *"Wow, it was an American airliner that hit the Pentagon. It's a day of national tragedy, and we'll clean up the mess and then the ball will be in your court and Dick Myer's court."* [16]

—GEORGE BUSH

Wow man:
That's like heavy. Hey, have you tried any of this medical marijuana from Ashcroft's office? He like confiscated a ton of Tommy Chong's bongs, too.

Never learns:
Bush is still assuming the attacks are over. Every time a plane hits a building and kills people, the president believes it to be the last one.

Good luck with that:
Rumsfeld isn't going to share a court. He didn't even want to share his time during the attacks. He once stabbed a man for using the last dab of Brillcreem.

Deadly tennis match:
Switching courts? What is this game and who had the ball up until now?

10:03 AM

Flight 93
Crashes In Pennsylvania

From The 9/11 Commission Report

At 10:00:26, a passenger in the background said, "In the cockpit. If we don't we'll die!" Sixteen seconds later, a passenger yelled, "Roll it!" Jarrah (hijacker) stopped the violent maneuvers at about 10:01:00 and said, "Allah is the greatest! Allah is the greatest!" He then asked another hijacker in the cockpit, "Is that it? I mean, shall we put it down?" to which the other replied, "Yes, put it in it, and pull it down. Pull it down!" The hijackers remained at the controls but must have judged that the passengers were only seconds from overcoming them. The airplane headed down; the control wheel was turned hard to the right. The airplane rolled onto its back, and one of the hijackers began shouting "Allah is the greatest. Allah is the greatest." With the sounds of the passenger counterattack continuing, the aircraft plowed into an empty field in Shanksville, Pennsylvania, at 580 miles per hour, about 20 minutes flying time from Washington, D.C.

Jarrah's objective was to crash his airliner into symbols of the American Republic, the Capitol or the White House. He was defeated by the alerted, unarmed passengers of United 93.

—9/11 COMMISSION

The attacks are over. President Bush is still wiping fog from his eyes.

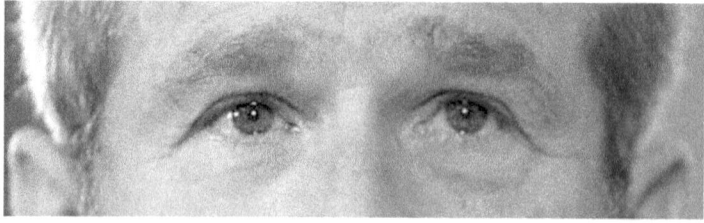

Review

9:30-10:03 am

Another 33 Minutes Shot To Hell

Fog, fog and more fog. The president continues his resolve to do nothing, citing an overabundance of information swirling around his brain.

Flight 77 slams into the Pentagon—hundreds die.

The vice president is moved to safety as a suicide plane bears down on D.C. The unimportant people are evacuated after the Pentagon is hit—the ones who are still alive.

In less than 30 minutes, with only cell phones to get information from the ground, the passengers aboard Flight 93 figured out the hijackers plot to intentionally crash the plane and kill innocents on the ground. With no complaints about the fog or the lack of information, they fight their attackers, as is the custom in America.

With all of the resources of the United States government at his fingertips, it takes President George W. Bush two hours after the hijacking of the Flight 11 to figure out what's going on and order any action to defend this country.

Pathetic.

There are a finite number of things that only the President of the United States has the power to do. One of them is to order the shoot-down of a commercial aircraft when it accidentally or intentionally threatens lives on the ground. George Bush did not bother to learn that part of his job.

In A Competent-Informed-Smart-Brave Leader World

Fortunately, the president has prepared his staff and the government agencies under his control for a possible hijacking or terrorist attack. He ordered all departments to call him immediately if anything the least bit out of the ordinary happens. It stands to reason that the greatest leader in American history should be in charge during the first moments of a crisis to nip it in the bud. Who else has the power to cut through the red tape and make things happen almost instantly? Brownie?

So, before the president left the hotel on the morning of 9/11, he received a call. "Mr. President, there's a hijacking in progress. Flight 11…it's a commercial airliner." The time is 8:25 am.

The president has increased security at the airports in response to all of the threats, and not in the sissified way of politely asking the airlines to please be careful—but with real government professionals. Unfortunately, it appears someone has found a seam and slipped through our defenses.

This sounds familiar, the wise and informed president thought. I've seen plenty of intelligence suggesting that al Qaeda has designs on hijacking American airliners. If those nasty evildoers are involved, this probably means the ruthless barbarians have plans to pull off something big and deadly—that's their MO. It's not in their nature to leave survivors.

Naturally, Mr. Bush is prepared. He's been reading the daily reports, paying attention during briefings and doing a vast amount of studying on his own. He knows his job. He's going to put in a full four years. No bankers hours, long weekends and five week vacations for him—not when there are so many things to learn. He's not about to let the "bureaucracy" filter what goes into his brain. After all, the protection of the American people is his most solemn duty and not to be taken lightly. George Bush isn't going to delegate the defense of our country to underlings and corporations. Finally, we have a president whose actions match his rhetoric.

"Get me Rumsfeld," he barks.

"Hello, Donny? Yea…say a plane has been hijacked and something doesn't smell right. It could be al Qaeda. They had thoughts of killing me with a suicide plane full of explosives during the G-8 Summit in Genoa a couple months back and I doubt they've retired. Anyway, we can't tell what's coming next, so button everything up. Yea, the whole dang country—and don't try to skip any states this time. Send the air guys, ground troops—everybody. Get some F-16's on the butt of that Flight 11. Nothing gets touched, you hear me? This is no time to start saving gas. I know you don't like interruptions …hey, hey, hey; I don't want to hear any witty banter, just do it! That's an order! Yeah, well screw you, too!"

Due to the high volume of threats during the summer, the president has maintained a high state of alert throughout the government, including fighter planes at the ready near all major cities. Within minutes, jets are on patrol over the entire country in case something develops. Two F-16's are trying to catch up to the hijacked plane. Hopefully, George W. Bush's careful preparations and hands-on leadership can save lives…

CHAPTER SEVEN

My
Little Runaway

"But the real man never lets fear of death overpower his honor, his sense of duty to his country and his innate manhood."
—GENERAL GEORGE PATTON D-DAY SPEECH

The attacks were over by the time Air Force One reached cruising altitude and Bush had blown all of his chances to act, so it didn't really matter where the president went. Nevertheless, his retreat was cowardly and caused embarrassment for the manly Chief Executive, so excuses were needed.

Exit Strategy

President Couldn't Communicate Until Reaching Air Force One
Favorite Snoopy telephone on board

> *"The best thing to do is exercise caution and to get the president to a position where he can be in communications with his team. And you don't have to be looking at each other to be in communication. You just have to be in communication."* [1]

—GEORGE BUSH

Bullshit:
The president was never out of communication with his crack "team."
Bush had a secure phone available at all times. The suggestion that he
needed to run away in order to communicate is a lie.

Exodus:
Caution? Bush didn't exercise any
caution when he heard the World
Trade Center had been hit. A
photo-op won out over the
defense of the country in that
brain teaser. Even when the second
plane hit and he was absolutely
"positive" the country was under
attack, the president showed no
concern for any life but his own.

Risking One's Life For A Noble Cause Bush Has Heard Of It...He Just Won't Do It

*"They died in a just cause for
defending freedom and they have
not died in vain."*

—GEORGE BUSH,
TALKING ABOUT THE
MEN AND WOMEN WHO HAVE GIVEN
THEIR LIVES FOR OTHERS.

❖ ❖ ❖

Braveheart

President Needs
To Be Removed From Immediate Threat

There's nothing worse than losing a hapless cowardly leader—with beady eyes

> *"I knew full well that I had made the absolutely right decision and
> history would record that. When the president is under threat, one
> thing for the good of the country is you want to remove the president
> from the immediate threat. There's nothing worse for a country having
> been attacked than a destabilized presidency. It would make matters
> a lot worse."* [2]

—GEORGE BUSH

What an ass:
George is so special—he had to run away and leave the second graders behind for the good of the country. Whatever would become of the country if George Bush wasn't around to stand on the rubble after an attack is over? If he is lucky, history will overlook the whole disgraceful episode.

Phony flee:
Bush also needs to be kept from making any decisions if he thinks he was under an immediate threat in Florida.

Not that stable to begin with:
A free range chicken with very limited skills is at the helm—we would get by, somehow.

Life Imitates Art—George Imitates George

Robin's Mother:
That's the coward that left us to die!

George Costanza:
I...was trying to lead the way. We needed a leader! Someone to lead the way to safety.

Robin:
But you yelled "get out of my way!"

George:
Because! Because, as the leader...if I die...then all hope is lost! Who would lead? The clown? Instead of castigating me, you should all be thanking me. What kind of a topsy-turvy world do we live in, where heroes are cast as villains? Brave men as cowards?

—SEINFELD
EPISODE NO. 84 "THE FIRE" [3]

"That's what this war is about is our way of life, and our way of life is worth losing lives for." [4]

—DONALD RUMSFELD

These Kids Look Like Survivors

Chief Of Staff: Air Force One Safe Environment
Elementary school unsafe—children might be OK, though—probably

> *I was intent on getting the president to a safe environment where he had good communications, and by definition, that was Air Force One at that particular moment. So we were anxious to get to Air Force One. As we were heading to Air Force One, we did hear about the Pentagon attack, and we also learned, what turned out to be a mistake, but we learned that the Air Force One package could in fact be a target."* [5]
>
> —ANDREW CARD

Finicky:
Bush had a room set up for him at the school with secure telephones. Communication equipment follows the president wherever he goes. What's so special about the phones on the plane?

Run towards the light:
If Air Force One was a target, why go to it? The hotel where Bush stayed on the 10th and left less than an hour ago was outfitted with a surface to air missile battery, an AWACS plane was overhead and the coast guard patrolled the shoreline. Call in some additional air support to protect the school and do the same for the rest of the country.

This chair is too soft:
Mayor Giuliani set up shop in the middle of New York to manage the crisis and seemed to do OK, but Goldilocks W. Bush can't find anywhere in the state of Florida, a thousand miles away from the attacks, to operate.

Falter Skalter

"The terrorists do not understand America. The American people do not falter under threat—and we will not allow our future to be determined by car bombers and assassins."

—GEORGE BUSH, JUNE 28, 2005,
EXPLAINING HIS THEORY ON NOT
FALTERING UNDER THREAT.

Protect The Queen

Card: Constitution Requires President To Stay In Safe Environment
Not the United States Constitution, though

> *"It was imperative that we understand that president has to stay in a safe environment where he has good communications, and that's what our Constitution requires. I mean, because only the president can make the toughest of decisions, and you know the tough decisions that were put on the president's desk. Should the military have the authority to shoot down a jet—commercial jetliner? That decision to be made by surrogates? It's a decision to be made by the president."* [6]

—ANDREW CARD

Heavily varnished:
Andy Card intentionally confuses his imaginary "Card Amendment" with the "line of succession," which dictates who is next in line for the office if something happens to the president. Dick's on deck...Denny's in the hole.

Permanent Static:
You can put Bush wherever you want, but without a gibberish interpreter, the communications still aren't going to be good.

Egocentric:
The president could have ordered the defense of the country before he ran away. Some of the suicide planes were in the air long enough to launder a load of $100 bills.

Ignorance:
It's true. Only the president has the authority to make the "toughest of decisions," like ordering the shoot-down of an airliner. But he didn't do it. George Bush couldn't make the needed decision on 9/11 because he didn't know it was his responsibility.

Open Book Test

"The real test of a leader is what he or she does under fire—Bush conferred with Cheney every 30 minutes." [7]

—CAROLYN B. THOMPSON
AND JAMES W. WARE
"THE LEADERSHIP GENIUS OF
GEORGE W. BUSH"

Bush logic:
The terrorists are in the sky—let's go up there!

9:33 AM

Passengers on Flight 93 learn about the attacks on the World Trade Center.

They Hate Our Freedom
To Call Collect

Advisor Can't Reach Air Force One
President took phone off the hook to get a little peace and quiet—jeezus!

> *"And the military operator came back to me and in a voice that, to me, sounded very shaken said, 'Ma'am, I'm sorry, we can't reach Air Force One.'"* [8]

—Karen Hughes on 60 Minutes II

Mixed signals:
Oh, so now the communications suck. Karen Hughes, who has played "Jenny" to George's "Forrest" for many years, tries to deflect criticism of the president's inability to give orders on 9/11 by blaming poor communications. Curiously, people on the hijacked planes were able to reach people on the ground with regular cell phones.

Two calling birds:
The president needed to be on Air Force One because of the good communications, but the poor communications on Air Force One are one of the excuses for Bush's ineptitude. It's a bullshit twofer.

Hit The Road Jack

Cheney: Presidential Responsibility Was To Run Away
Bush's safety takes priority over defense of country—it was in incredibly fine print in their campaign ads

> *"Well, we erred on the side of, I'd say, responsibility. The—when something like this happens, we've got certain obligations and responsibilities you've got to carry out. And those took priority. They did for the president. They did for me. Also with modern communications— I mean, the president was in touch with me throughout the day. We talked repeatedly. He made some key decisions that were very important to the operation."* [9]

—DICK CHENEY, MEET THE PRESS 9/16/2001

Error Jordan:
The "erred on the side of responsibility" president; when trouble breaks out, he'll be there—as soon as he finds a good place to hide. Soon, the president will come to be known as George "Aftermath" Bush in recognition of his ability to show up three days late for any crisis—and hug the stuffing out of several Rove planted survivors for the cameras.

Operation Petticoat:
The "operation" didn't involve defending the country, but the president made some key decisions—he's such a nice boy.

Write if you get work:
Bush stayed in touch with Cheney? So what? Did the president need someone to break a tie? Turkey Clubs or Cobb Salads for lunch?

The Sacrifice Of Others—Is A Sacrifice He Is Willing To Make

"The work in Iraq is difficult and dangerous. Like most Americans, I see the images of violence and bloodshed. Every picture is horrifying—and the suffering is real. Amid all this violence, I know Americans ask the question: Is the sacrifice worth it? It is worth it, and it is vital to the future security of our country."

—GEORGE BUSH

Eye Of The Tiger

**President Made Decision
To Be In Position To Make Decisions**
Plans to stay in Nebraska permanently to save time

> *"I believe I took the—I know—I don't believe, I know I took the appropriate actions as the Commander in Chief, to be in a position to be able to make the decisions necessary for our government to handle the crisis."*
>
> —GEORGE BUSH SEPTEMBER 13, 2001

Telecommuter:
Until Stanley Steadfast gets 2000 miles away, don't expect him to do anything. There are phones wherever the president goes—he was even visiting with some of his pals on several of them, but that's the rule—Bush doesn't do any deciding, defending or ciphering until he's at least a half a continent away from harm—even if it's fictional harm.

Pass the popcorn:
Bush didn't handle the crisis, so much as peek at it through his fingers.

Captain America

Bush Proud Of Decision To Run Away
Not talking about Viet Nam this time—or that Jagermeister related incident at the Houston Marriot involving that wiry bellboy

> *"At any rate, I knew I had a job to do. And I was quoted in the press the other day as saying I haven't regretted one thing I've decided. And that's the truth. Every decision I made, I stand by. And I'm proud of the decisions I've made."*
>
> —GEORGE BUSH DECEMBER 4, 2001

Cowardly braggart:
The diva didn't do one solitary thing on 9/11—and he's delighted to crow about his bold feat of nothingness.

Pathological:
Bush never regrets anything—except for not legally changing his name to
"Carmello" before it was snapped up

Want To Have A Beer
With Him Now?

Bush Desperately Wanted To Come Back To DC
And he really wanted to be in the infantry in '68—dang the luck

> *"I wanted to come back to Washington, but the circumstances were
> such that it was just impossible for the Secret Service or the national
> security team to clear the way for Air Force One to come back."* [10]

—GEORGE BUSH 60 MINUTES II

Isn't that precious:
George still doesn't know that he's in charge.

Mr. Roboto

Fleischer: Threat Real And Credible
Fake caller also said Bush would be greeted as a liberator in Louisiana

> *"Because the information that we had was real and credible about
> Air Force One. And the manner in which Air Force One operated
> maintained the security of Air Force One at all times. And that
> also is one of the reasons why Air Force One did not come back to
> Andrews, where some people thought it would."* [11]

—ARI FLEISCHER

The fugitive:
Air Force One first landed in Louisiana, but Bush complained about the
humidity—frizzy hair—so the presidential entourage split for Nebraska.

Hold Me Back

Bush: I'm Coming Back!

President considers "country under attack" the perfect time to make a meaningless symbolic gesture

> *"It was brief because I was being pushed to get off the phone and get out of the West Wing. They were hurrying me off the phone with the president and I just said, he said, 'I'm coming back' and we said, 'Mr. President, that may not be wise.'"*[12]

—CONDI RICE

He's there in spirit:

With so little to brag about, the administration takes every opportunity to inject some bravery into the president's speech, if not his actions. Condi is being evacuated as she converses with the president, because a hijacked plane is headed towards D.C., but he still doesn't get the drift and do something.

Drama Queen

Hughes: Crisis Worse If President Harmed

Honor of risking one's life for just cause reserved for enlisted men and women

> *"When Air Force One took off, I thought it was headed for Washington; Dan and I didn't know that the vice president, Andy Card and Condi Rice had recommended the president stay away from Washington because we didn't know exactly what we were dealing with, and they knew this crisis would be even worse if something happened to the president."*[13]

—KAREN HUGHES

Hair splitting:

Worse? Bush didn't lift a finger to save one life—how could the crisis have been worse?

Foresight:
Who would protect us from the yellowcake and stock FEMA with an Algonquin table of half-wits if Bush weren't around?

❖ ❖ ❖

He's Hearing Alarm Bells Now

Caution Must Be Taken
For him

> *"The President is looking forward to returning to Washington. He understands at a time like this, caution must be taken; and he wants to get to back to Washington."* [14]

—ARI FLEISCHER

True grit:
Women and children last. If there is only one survivor, please let it be George.

Whew!

Terrorists Tried To Kill President On 9/11
Got within 938 miles—too close for comfort

> *"After all, they [Secret Service agents] were guarding the president on a day when ruthless and cunning terrorists were obviously trying to kill him."* [15]

—BILL SAMMON

Boot scootin' boogier:
As one of the lackeys assigned to paint a handsome face on a water buffalo's butt, Sammon is only doing his job, but at least he could have tried to come up with something plausible.

> *"Once a leader gives up,*
> *then everybody else gives up,*
> *and there's no hope."*
> —RUDOLPH GIULIANI "LEADERSHIP"

CHAPTER EIGHT

The President
Gives An Order

10:15–10:20 AM

*"The truth is, you can't fake expertise. People pick up that kind
of pretense right away and will take advantage of your
ignorance or dismiss you outright as a dilettante."*
—RUDOLPH GIULIANI

Doing nothing hasn't worked out for Team Bush during the first 90
minutes of the attacks, so Vice President Cheney orders the president to
order the Air Force to shoot-down suicide planes. Then Bush orders the
vice president to give the order. The attacks were over, but the president
didn't know that, so he scores a few points—as many as you get for
making a 10-foot jump shot two hours after the final buzzer.

Nearly three years later, both men would find out from the 9/11 Commission
that their shoot-down order didn't even make it to the pilots. It was the
one thing Bush did that came remotely close to leadership on 9/11 and he
screwed it up. Even Harriet was disappointed.

The Contemplation

Dynamic Duo

VP: Air Cover No Good Without Orders
No more patrols—just scramble and start shooting

> *"VP recalled feeling that it did no good to establish a CAP
> (Combat Air Patrol) unless the pilots had instructions to shoot
> if the plane would not divert. He said the president signed off on that
> concept. The president said he remembered such a conversation, and
> that it reminded him of when he had been an interceptor pilot."*
>
> —911 COMMISSION REPORT

Bullshit:
There were fighter jets already in the air waiting for orders—any orders.
The VP insinuates that he and president were ahead of the situation,
instead of 90 minutes behind. Dick can be quite the chubby little weasel.

Frozen flounder:
Bush has the power to unleash the
Air Force at any time. No concept
needed to be revealed during a
heart to heart with Uncle Dick.

Up Is Down— Just Say The Opposite Of Reality And All Will Be Fine

*"Making a decision in time is proba-
bly even more important than making
the decision. We've all known leaders who
made decisions too late or have allowed
time to make the decisions for them. This
president will make a decision in time
for it to be implemented well. That
requires courage."* [1]

—ANDREW CARD, EVIDENTLY STONED
OUT OF HIS MIND, TO RONALD
KESSLER, AUTHOR OF "A MATTER OF
CHARACTER, INSIDE THE WHITE
HOUSE OF GEORGE W. BUSH"

We Go To War
With The President We Have...

Bush And VP
Discuss Shooting Down Hijacked Airliners

After several minutes, a full blown meeting breaks out—with pie charts and fruit pies

> *"As the planes track toward Washington, a discussion begins about whether to shoot them down. I discussed it with the president. 'Are we prepared to order our aircraft to shoot down these airliners that have been hijacked?'"* [2]

—DICK CHENEY

Twin geeks:

No discussion is needed—the protocol is clear. The Vice President isn't even in the chain of command. The decision is for the president to make. Hold hands at the movies.

Foggy bottom boys:

Smoke them down, maybe? What's the holdup? Shoot the planes down or let them hit their targets.

Yellow Jell-O:

Not too crisp—the conversation takes place more than 30 minutes after Flight 77 hits the Pentagon. Horse...barn, and so-forth.

"The President Took Strong Action To Protect Our Country."

—GOVERNOR GEORGE PATAKI

Doubtful:

Would George Sr. have called Dan Quayle?

The Decision

Get The Aircraft Carrier Ready For Snapshots

Bush Said "Yes"
"It was the happiest day of my life" remembers VP

"He said yes. It was my advice. It was his decision." [3]

—DICK CHENEY

Little Richard:
Cheney can't resist taking credit for an obvious decision made after the attacks were over and confirming Bush as an ignorant doofus. The VP is sent to an undisclosed location soon after.

Patent pending:
The vice president gave the advice, yes; but nothing was invented—the procedures were already in place to deal with such threat. Was the president just feigning ignorance to wrangle some more "us" time with big Dick?

The Wimperer Strikes Back

President Authorizes Shoot-Down
Concludes submissive hands-off policy regarding suicide planes

"Shortly after we took off, the President authorized the military to shoot down any civilian aircraft that was deemed a threat." [4]

—ARI FLEISCHER

Ari time:
The thumbs up to defend the nation didn't come from Bush for another 15 or 20 minutes after Air Force One took off.

Hoodwinkish:
The president didn't authorize the military to do anything himself. Vice President "go f___ yourself" Cheney did the honors, and then botched the order, anyway.

Fat Catlike Reflexes

VP's Reaction Time Quick And Decisive
Especially for a person with no discernable physique

> *His reaction time was described by Scooter Libby as quick and decisive, "in about the time it takes a batter to decide to swing." The Vice President authorized fighter aircraft to engage the inbound plane.*

> —9/11 COMMISSION REPORT

Foul ball:
The president instructed Cheney to give the order—it didn't come to the VP in the heat of the moment, but good sucking up by the future felon. And it took Lardsky and Putz an hour and a half to figure out a protocol that already existed. Nothing swift about it.

The Protocol

The Mystery
Of The Secret Protocol

Bush Quickly Realized Nation Under Attack
Only an hour after being told "America is under attack"

> *"You bet," Bush told the VP. The president told me later that this wasn't a difficult decision to make, "once I realized there was a protocol...because again, I now realized we're under attack. This is a war. And it took me no time to realize it was a war."* [5]

> —GEORGE BUSH TO BILL SAMMON

No actionable intellect:
Card said, "America is under attack" at 9:05 am and the protocol
was in place to deal with hijacked and suicide planes. The only piece
missing was a leader who knew his job.

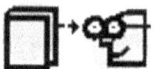

Hijack Protocol

*"And the Department of Defense has had various understandings with the
FAA whereby when someone squawks "hijack," they have an arrangement
with the Department of Defense that the military would send an airplane
up and monitor the flight, but certainly in a hijack situation, did not
have authority to shoot down a plane that was being hijacked."*

—DONALD RUMSFELD TO 9/11 COMMISSION

Hijack Protocol II

*"Prior to making any judgment, every effort is made to dissuade an air-
plane to go into any area that's prohibited, for example. And there are
all kinds of ways that that's done. It's done through radio communications, it's done through hand signals, it's done through flying in front of
an airplane. So there's all kinds of things that are done in advance, as well
as checking various IFF procedures to see if there's an abnormal signal."* [6]

—DONALD RUMSFELD DoD NEWS BRIEFING 9/27/2001

Shoot-Down Protocol

*"Prior to 9/11, it was understood that an order to shoot down a commercial
aircraft would have to be issued by the National Command Authority (the
President and Secretary of Defense)."*

—9/11 COMMISSION REPORT

Dripping With Protocol

Presidential Decision, Says General Myers
Now if we can just find the little rascal

> *"Remembering my days as the North American Aerospace Defense Command Commander, and we had this Lear jet that Payne Stewart, the golfer, was on, and for some reason they all became incapacitated, that issue came up then, and that's why I knew it was not a decision that the military or the Department of Defense could make, it had to go all of the way to—to the—to presidential level to get that kind of decision because there were American citizens on board."* [7]

—GENERAL RICHARD MYERS

Oh, Who Are We Kidding?

Myers: Presidential Authority Needed
So the Vice President is called—maybe he will know where junior is

> *"And knowing that it was a U.S. airliner with Americans on board, the authority to shoot something, an airliner down that was going to create a, commit a hostile act on sites or forces on the ground, requires presidential-level authority. And so the Secretary of Defense wound up calling the Vice President in this case who authorized that if it was necessary."* [8]

—GENERAL MYERS

General idea:
So...now the Defense Secretary is calling Cheney for shoot-down authorization? Doubtful. Donny would rather have a peace sign branded on his forehead than ask the VP for permission to blow something up.

Fairy tale:
Rumsfeld didn't call Dick, and the vice president doesn't have the authority to shoot down a weather balloon—unless it's robbing the Cheney McMansion.

False Idol Award Winner

Only Cheney Could Conceive Of Shoot-Down Order
President and Defense Secretary even dumber than earlier thought

> *"Only someone with his experience in the Defense Department could have conceived on the spot of such a drastic but necessary measure."* [9]
>
> —RONALD KESSLER "A MATTER OF CHARACTER"

Immaculate conception:
The author of the ironically named "A Matter of Character," Ronald Kessler isn't ashamed to openly worship the Buddha shaped vice president and his mystical powers.

Dick free:
If Richard Cheney never existed, planes would be crashing into buildings without resistance for eternity.

Secretary's day:
Poor Donny gets snubbed again. Rumsfeld has been the Secretary of Defense twice.

The Self Analysis

The Commander-in-Chief gives an order way too late and the command to shoot-down suicide planes doesn't even get to the fighter pilots. But, since it was the only thing Bush did on 9/11, it makes the highlight reels and is a very proud moment for the president and his disciples.

The Latest Generation

Tough Call For President Says Rove
It was right in the middle of nap time, but he gutted it out

"At times during the day, my handwriting wasn't easy to read, but at about 10:20, he went forward from his office into the private cabin in front of it and took a phone call and came back in and said that he had talked to the Vice President and to the Secretary of Defense and gave the authorization that military could shoot down any planes not under control of their crews that were nearing critical targets. Just the horror of having to make that decision, yet he was calm and even, you know. You do with a great—it was a great, tough call, but it was one that had to be made and he made it." [10]

—KARL ROVE

When liars collide:
Bush didn't talk to the Defense Secretary. That would have made sense. Did the president lie to Rove or is Karl enhancing the story on his own?

Good little soldier:
If it was the right thing to do at 10:20 am, it would have been the right thing to do an hour and a half before.

Clear skies:
Horror? Maybe after brunch. There was nothing close to horror in the private cabin of the president. Bush's failure to make the "great, tough call" earlier, when it could have actually helped save lives only caused needless pain and suffering for more people and their families.

To Defend Or Not To Defend... Finally The Question

VP: Shoot-Down Order Tough Decision
Much harder than doing business with Saddam in the 90's—he was a peach

"Well, the—I suppose the toughest decision was this question of whether or not we would intercept incoming commercial aircraft."

—DICK CHENEY, MEET THE PRESS 9/16/2001

But Bush says:
"But it was an easy decision to make…"

Stumper:
Stop a suicide plane from killing thousands of innocent people on the ground—or not? Can't get much more "clarity" than that.

Is Pepsi OK?
It was the only relevant decision Bush made on 9/11 and he screwed it up.

He's Very Wise Indeed…Chalabi-like

President Had No Choice, Says Rice
Except to project strength and calm, but that just gave him Super Bowl fever

> *"For the president, I think a very difficult decision, but a decision that, at some level, he had no choice but to make that decision. And so while it was difficult, in one sense, I'm sure that, in another sense, it must have seemed to him that he had no choice, but to do that."* [11]
>
> —CONDI RICE

Eureka:
Exactly. Bush had no other correct choice. Unfortunately, the president didn't know it was his decision to make. It's probably in the manual some-where—some reading will be required, though…or some books on tape.

Sad Sack:
Poor George. All the president had to do was follow the common sense and documented procedure for dealing with such a threat. He's no hero.

The Weakest Link

Bush: "I Didn't Hesitate"
Has absolutely no freaking idea what "hesitate" means

> *"That's a sobering moment to order your own combat aircraft to shoot down your own civilian aircraft. But it was an easy decision to make given the—given the fact that we had learned that a commercial aircraft was being used as a weapon. I say easy decision, it was, I didn't hesitate, let me put it that way. I knew what had to be done."* [12]

> —GEORGE BUSH

Narcolepsy?
At the very latest, Bush learned aircraft were being used as weapons at 9:05 am…75 minutes have passed since then.

Boastful buffoon:
He's so full of crap. Of course it's an easy decision to make, if you wait until the attacks are over.

Puppet:
Bush still needed Cheney to tell him what to do. Who knows who told the vice president?

And We Would Do It Again By Golly

Opportunity Didn't Knock

**VP: Government Justified
In Shooting Down New York Bound Planes**
No kidding

> *"If we had had combat air patrol up over New York and we'd had the opportunity to take out the two aircraft that hit the World Trade Center, would we have been justified in doing that? I think absolutely we would have. Now, it turned out we did not have to execute on that authorization."* [13]

> —DICK CHENEY, MEET THE PRESS 9/16/2001

Eunuch:
Who's The Boss? Does the president want patrols—or fighter planes on alert? Does he want F-16's scrambled? Any date, 24 hours a day, all the Commander-in-Chief has to do is snap his fingers to make things happen. George Bush doesn't have to wait for a requisition to land on his desk before making a decision. If the president wants New York protected, he has the power. If the president orders it, the pilots will fly upside down for the whole time. His authority even exceeds that of the Mayor of New Orleans.

Wish Upon a Star

No Fighter Planes On Alert Near New York
Can only afford protection for the really big cities—and beloved ranch

> *"Well, the president will, I'm sure, make a decision, if those circumstances arise again. It's a presidential-level decision, and the president made, I think, exactly the right call in this case, to say, "I wished we'd had combat air patrol up over New York."* [14]

> —DICK CHENEY, MEET THE PRESS 9/16/2001

Responsibility:
Yep, it's an executive decision alright…too bad the president didn't know that. He may need a few more lessons.

Movie moment:
In the 1996 movie "Executive Decision," terrorists seize control of an airliner with the intention of detonating a chemical bomb in the United States. Kurt Russell and a band of commandos must deactivate the bomb and rescue the passengers. If they can't do it before the plane reaches U.S. airspace, the president will be forced to make an "executive decision" and shoot down the aircraft.

Specialization Run Amok

**Pilots Not Trained
To Shoot Down Commercial Airliners**
Too big

> *"Were we ready for it? I think the agencies responded very well once it happened. I think the courage and the bravery of the men and women of New York, for example, the first responders, if you will, fire and rescue teams, many of whom gave their lives when the towers collapsed, was superb. I don't think you can take anything away from them. But the problem you have here—I mean, if you think about it from the standpoint of aircraft—do we train our pilots to shoot down commercial airliners filled with American civilians? No. That's not a mission they've ever been given before. Now we've got to think about that."* [15]

> —Dick Cheney, Meet the Press 9/16/2001

Scapegoat:
USAF pilots don't need to be specially trained to shoot down a jumbo jet—they will follow orders. The president fails and the VP puts the blame on the pilots, who actually did their jobs. Patronizing, condescending, pretentious, lying jackass.

Indifference?
If the VP had been doing the assigned reading, he would have known that the use of airliners as weapons was a well considered possibility. So, yes, it might be a good time to start thinking about it.

It's the protocol stupid:
Cheney knows the decision to shoot down a passenger plane is a presidential call, but how did the protocol exist if no one had ever given it a thought?

Good heavens!
How will the F-16 pilots protect the president from large planes supposedly targeting Air Force One if they haven't been properly trained?

One Size Fits All

"The mission of the Air National Guard at the time was to protect the American coast. We were trained to shoot down other airplanes."

—GEORGE BUSH, "A CHARGE TO KEEP"

If We Have A Few Days To Get Ready

My Bologna Has A First Name...

Attack Too Unconventional For Military Response
We were expecting a Spanish armada style attack—they're all the rage on terror circuit

> *Mr. Bartlett, the White House spokesman, said that a swifter military response to the events of Sept. 11 would have been impossible because of "the unconventional nature of this attack." Even after the second Trade Center tower was hit, he said, "specific commands would have required much deeper knowledge of the [terrorist] operation that was under way."* [16]
>
> —WALL STREET JOURNAL

What a crock:
Is the White House saying that USAF pilots couldn't do the job if they were given the command, "protect [insert city and state needing protection here]?"

Black hole:
Deeper knowledge my butt. The terrorists didn't even try to fake anyone out. Just because Bush couldn't comprehend the "unconventional" nature of the attack as it unfolded doesn't make it complicated. Al Qaeda members bought tickets, hijacked airliners—exactly what they threatened to do, and went right for the most obvious targets.

Like lightning:
The military can act only as quickly as the leaders giving the orders. Our leader isn't too swift.

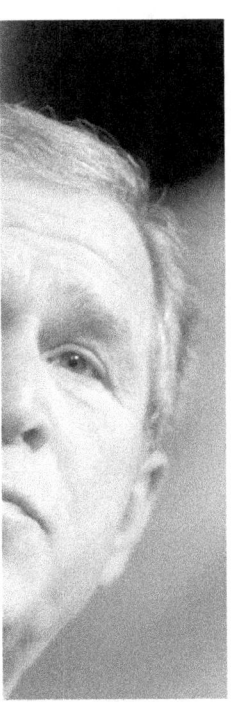

Concerned About The Unconventional And Yet... Still Surprised

"We have been deeply concerned, since I assumed my post with President Bush, about the so-called asymmetrical threats—the problems of the reality that people don't want to contest our armies, navies or air forces. They know they'll lose. What they can do, is use these asymmetrical threats of terrorism and chemical warfare and biological warfare, and ballistic missiles, and cruise missiles and cyber attacks." [17]

—DONALD RUMSFELD

Rumsfeld
And The Shoot-Down Order
Reality Version

10:39 AM

Heard It Through The Grapevine

VP Informs Rumsfeld Of Shoot-Down Order
Secretary starts twitching violently—temporarily unable
to make smartass remarks

> *"One of my first conversations during the conference call was with*
> *the Vice President. He informed me of the President's authorization*
> *to shoot down hostile aircraft coming toward Washington, D.C."* [18]

—DONALD RUMSFELD

Conscientious
Cognitive Consciousness

Rumsfeld Gains Situational Awareness
Other types of awareness still missing

> *"Secretary Rumsfeld told us he was just gaining situational awareness*
> *when he spoke to the Vice President at 10:39."*

—9/11 COMMISSION REPORT

Translation:
Had no clue.

Rumsfeld
And The Shoot-Down Order
Wishful Thinking Versions

Did these guys just make up the following scenarios or did someone from the White House feed the stories to them? By his own admission, the defense secretary was situationally stupid until 10:39 am and yet a number of accounts include him in the shoot-down order loop. Why the lies?

Surrounded By An Inferno He Was

Bush Conveys Order To Defense Secretary
Chain of Command now VP to President to Defense Secretary

> *"The vice president urged him to authorize military planes to shoot down any commercial airliners that might be controlled by the hijackers. Bush called Rumsfeld, who had elected to stay in the burning Pentagon, and conveyed the order."* [19]

> —RONALD KESSLER "A MATTER OF CHARACTER"

Chance to Tinkers to Evers:
17, 8, 35. Cher and Sonny. It's just not the right order.

The Professor & Mr. Howell

President Explains Order To Rumsfeld
That would have made for an interesting conversation

> *"The president then explained the shoot-down order to Donald Rumsfeld, who was still at the burning Pentagon."* [20]

> —BILL SAMMON

Later:
Bush tells Raphael Palmeiro how to hit a curveball.

Thumbs Up

Bush Approves Order
At secretary's suggestion, adds Halliburton cheese for an extra $25 million

> *"If the plane continued heading toward what was seen as a significant target with apparently hostile intent, the U.S. pilot would have the authority to shoot it down. With Bush's approval, Rumsfeld passed the order down the chain of command."* [21]

—DAN BALZ AND BOB WOODWARD, WASHINGTON POST

Let's Review

Shoot-Down Order

An hour and a half after the first attack and 20 minutes after passengers force the terrorists to dive Flight 93 into a Pennsylvania field, the president swings into action and orders the shoot-down of suicide planes.

The order never gets to the pilots.

CHAPTER NINE

High Alert
45,000 Feet High

"Why is this man in the White House? The majority of Americans did not vote for him. Why is he there? And I tell you this morning that he's in the White House because God put him there for a time such as this." [1]
—Lt. General William G. Boykin

As with most remembrances of the president's day, recollections vary on when or if Bush put the military on high alert. Common sense would suggest that the military was pretty alert when fighter jets took off at 8:46 am, but the president wanted to do it himself, so they called everyone back and let the little guy give the order right after his morning treat.

But, like the shoot-down order, it was way late—Bush was on his way to Louisiana by the time he deduced the military might be useful. God was shaking her head.

10:20 AM

Everyone Was At Woodstock, Too

Bush Orders Military To High Alert
Only 48th person to do so—including that smartass Haig

"After two more conversations with Cheney and a briefing from a CIA official, the president instructed Rumsfeld to order all U.S. military bases, domestic and on foreign soil, to raise their threat alert status from normal, which is the lowest of five levels, to Delta, the highest." [2]

—BILL SAMMON

Gloves are off now:
After being told, "America is under attack," in the most unfiltered, un-varnished way possible, it only takes the president another 75 minutes to put the military on alert.

Or Was It The General?

The Wall Street journal reported that Air Force General Richard Myers, acting head of the Joint Chiefs of Staff on 9/11 gave the order to raise the military's alert status to Defcon III shortly after the Pentagon was struck. [3]

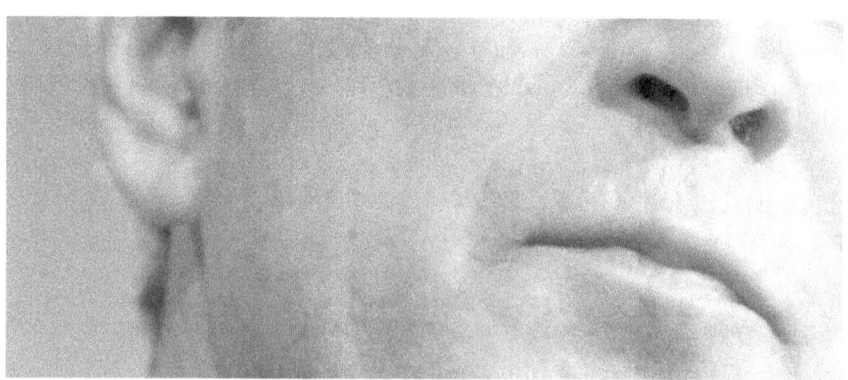

No Wait!
Better Stay The Course

President Puts
Military On Alert As One Of First Acts
Waits until attacks are over to get a good read on the situation

> *"And so, I got on the phone from Air Force One, asking to find out the facts. You've got to understand, Jordan, during this period of time, there were all kinds of rumors floating around. Some of them were erroneous. Obviously—for example, there was a news report saying that the State Department had been attacked. I needed to know what the facts were. But I knew I needed to act. I knew that if the nation's under attack, the role of the Commander-In-Chief is to respond forcefully to prevent other attacks from happening. And so, I've talked to the Secretary of Defense; one of the first acts I did was to put our military on alert."* [4]

—GEORGE BUSH

Rubbernecker:
Evidently, Bush can't put the military on alert until he first hears what's been blown up.

Poor Jordan:
He's done been misled. Bush gives the impression that he was on Air Force One and looking for information shortly after the attacks began, when in fact he didn't even get on the plane until an hour after the first tower was hit—and then took another 30 minutes after he boarded to give an order.

**Don't forget about
the fog:**
Bush couldn't do anything due to
the dew.

Wake Me Up
Before You Go Go

"According to an FBI spokesman,
the CONPLAN was activated
quickly and most federal agencies
went into action without input
from the president, because the
situation was widely known due
to the TV coverage." [5]

—WALL STREET JOURNAL

❖ ❖ ❖

Long Fuse

Rumsfeld Recommends Raising Force Protection Level
Finally pissed off

> *"Upon my return from the crash site and before going to the Executive
> Support Center (ESC), I had one or more calls in my office, one of
> which I believe was with the President. I left the ESC and went to the
> National Military Command Center where General Dick Myers, then
> Vice Chairman of the Joint Chiefs of Staff, had just returned from
> Capitol Hill. We discussed and I recommended to the President raising
> the U.S. Defense Condition level from 5 to 3, and increasing the
> Force Protection level." [6]*

—DONALD RUMSFELD, SPEAKING TO THE 9/11 COMMISSION

Whoa Rummy!
At the earliest…75 minutes after the first attack and 40 minutes after the
Pentagon is hit, the Secretary of Defense thinks it's perhaps time to defend
the country. Rumsfeld would also tell the Commission that he didn't even
reach situational awareness until 10:39—nearly two hours after the first attack.

Peyote?
Don talks to the president—at least he's pretty sure it was Bush. It was hard to tell through all the sobbing.

Wimp:
The Secretary of Defense doesn't need permission to raise the alert level.

On 9/11/2001, Rumsfeld said...
"We have in fact declared Force Protection Condition Delta and a condition of high alert—indeed, the highest alert. We did so **almost immediately** upon the attacks, and it is still in force." He lied. [7]

10:28 AM

The North Tower of the World Trade Center collapses.

> *"The fanatics who killed some 3,000 of our fellow Americans*
> *may have thought they could attack us with impunity—because*
> *terrorists had done so previously. But if the killers of September 11th*
> *thought we had lost the will to defend our freedom, they did not know*
> *America...and they did not know George W. Bush. "* [8]
> —DICK CHENEY, 2004 REPUBLICAN CONVENTION

CHAPTER TEN

Afternoon
Respite

"The amazing thing about this job, though,
is the job seems to follow you around."
—George Bush July 9, 2001

After the attacks were over, the president turned into quite the tiger, getting super tough, supposedly making big decisions right and left and acting very manly—the testosterone was pa-pa-palpable. It's hard to find a reference to any actual decisions, though—according to the president and his staff, he spent Tuesday afternoon mostly muttering about tin horns, bastards, and kicking asses.

Rain Man

President Bush
Spots A Pattern After Reaching Louisiana
Deductive skills surpass those of the ring tailed lemur

> *"There were still two international flights unaccounted for and Bush considered them potential missiles."* [1]

—Bill Sammon

Relaxed fit genes:
He laughs at jokes about a week later, too.

11:45 AM

Air Force One lands at Barksdale Air Force Base in Louisiana.

Driving Miss Daisy

Bush More Observant At Barksdale
Sedatives starting to wear off—dosage spiked for ride back to plane

> *"I was much more observant in Barksdale. I'll never forget getting in a car and going about 150 miles an hour. I thought the most dangerous part of the whole day was driving across the tarmac, these guys with guns strapped on them."* [2]
>
> —GEORGE BUSH

Not a morning person:
It's good to know Bush was starting to pay attention by the time he got to Louisiana. Maybe he shouldn't be working the first shift.

Chickenhawk battlefield:
The president is secured safely on a U.S. military base at mid-continent—the biggest green zone—ever. Hair-raising.

This Means War

The president figures out we're at war and everyone makes a big deal out of his deductive powers. Evidently, this obvious epiphany is the only contribution Bush needed to make to qualify for the 9/11 leadership banner, a tasteful "best cheerleader" plaque and a free hook-up to the Weather Channel.

Bored Game

Bush Instantly Recognizes Attacks As War
A little slow on recognizing the attacks as attacks—but that's really for the advanced players

> *"Two things struck me watching events in the early hours of September 11. One was the confusion and lack of facts. The other was the President's instant recognition that this was war and his determination to lead our nation in winning it."* [3]

—ARI FLEISCHER

Stroke of Genius:
Thousands are dead, the Twin Towers are in ruins and the Pentagon is on fire—even Ari was able to figure out the terminology. As Fleischer said, "If an attack on our country wasn't war, what was?" [4]

Teachers Pet

Bush Only 4th President
To Declare War On Terrorism
Lets al Qaeda slide on bombing of Navy ship Cole, but he's ready now

> *"And yet Clinton's successor was giving every indication that this time would be different. He immediately declared war on terrorism and did not wait for a federal indictment to conclude that bin Laden was the prime suspect."* [5]

—BILL SAMMON

Steely Man

Rove: President Knew We Were At War
Advisor uses custom-made Bush thesaurus to describe the chief's mild brain activity

> *"But it was steel and he was quiet, but it was very firm and it was very resolved and there was clarity. There was no confusion in his mind. He knew we were at war."* [6]

—KARL ROVE

> *"Unwarranted, unprovoked attacks against innocent American citizens is clearly an act of war, and one that requires that kind of national response and international response."* [7]

—JOHN McCAIN 9/11/2001

> *"This was an act of war against the United States."* [8]

—DAN QUAYLE 9/11/2001

❖ ❖ ❖

12:11 PM

The Soft Bigotry Of Low Expectations

Bush: Government Functioning Smoothly
Except for the death and destruction, the day has been a heckava success

"I think it's important for people to see the government is functioning, because the TV shows our nation has been blasted and bombed. The government is not chaotic. It's functioning smoothly. We're gonna get the bastards." [9]

—GEORGE BUSH

Low bar:
The country has been attacked by amateurs; thousands of people are dead and wounded, and Bush thinks the government is functioning smoothly.

Aunest Ari:
A trusted and loyal advisor disagrees. Fleischer says, "Even on Air Force One, in the hub of power and information, confusion was the order of the day." [10]

Not Us Personally, Of Course

Bush: We're Going To Kick Their Ass
Later decides to blow them up—some electrocuted for old times sake

"We're at war, Dick, we're going to find out who did this and kick their ass." [11]

—GEORGE BUSH

Oh, puleeze:
Everyone knows who's behind the attacks by now, so can we quit pretending it was such a surprise.

Stench:
Andy Card said, "Smells like Osama bin Laden to me" about the same time as Rumsfeld gained "situational awareness" a few hours ago. [12]

1:31 PM

Air Force One takes off from Louisiana. Too many hurricanes and poor people—who needs it?

2:00 PM

Wish You Were Here

President Concerned With Safety Of People
Will take everyone with him to Nebraska next time

> *"The President's concern is with the safety of people and with the families of those who lost their lives."* [13]

> —ARI FLEISCHER

Thanks for the card:
Some concern for the safety of other people would have been useful about five hours ago.

Huggy bear:
Bush would become proficient at extending condolences to the relatives and friends of dead Americans during his time in office.

2:30 PM

Based On Actual Events

Karen Hughes Makes Statement To Country
Only lies several times—not even close to a personal best

> *"While some federal buildings have been evacuated for security reasons and to protect our workers, your federal government continues to function effectively. We have a federal emergency*

*response plan, and at President Bush's direction, we are
implementing it. We began to implement it immediately after
the first attack in New York this morning. We contacted American
forces and embassies throughout the world and placed them on high
alert. The United States Secret Service immediately secured the
President, the Vice President and the Speaker of the House, and they
are all safe. They have also secured members of the national security
team, the President's Cabinet and senior staff. As you know, President
Bush was in Sarasota, Florida when the first attack occurred this
morning. Air Force One has now landed at Offutt Air Force Base in
Omaha, Nebraska, and the President is in a secure location. He is in
continuous communication with the Vice President and key members
of his Cabinet and national security team. Vice President Cheney and
our National Security Advisor, Condoleezza Rice, are in a secure
facility at the White House…"*

—Karen Hughes September 11, 2001

"My statement included all the information we had confidence in…" [14]

—Karen Hughes "Ten Minutes from Normal"

Lie:
The emergency response plan, the CONPLAN, was implemented long
before Bush even knew there was such a thing.

Selective service:
Was that the order? Evacuate "some" of the buildings! About 40 percent of
them should be enough. The people at the Pentagon might have appreciated
being on the list.

Elite retreat:
Vice President Cheney was moved to a bunker while Flight 77 was in the
air—but most others in the White House weren't evacuated until after the
plane hit the Pentagon.

Culture of his life:
If the president was immediately secured as Hughes described, why did he
leave the school for Omaha?

Collateral damage:
But, if the school wasn't safe, why were the children left behind?

Big time big deal:
When it comes to matters of defense, the Queen of England has as much authority as Vice President Cheney.

2:35 PM

"The number of casualties will be more than anyone can bear."

—Mayor Giuliani

Beauty School Drop-Out

Great Actions Were Happening Says Rove
2002, 2004 and 2006 election talking points falling together nicely

"There really was—I mean, you knew we were in the middle of a storm, but the President's demeanor was such that it sort of set the tone and that was just sort of quiet, firm, resolved, but you sensed the great actions that were happening around you." [15]

—Karl Rove, reciting the
"demeanor more important than results" talking points

More demeanor:
Getting a wee bit nauseous here.

Hair Was Literally Growing On The Concrete Walls

President, VP Strong And Decisive
Hughes impressed and amazingly sincere

"I was impressed by the strength and decisiveness I was witnessing as the vice president coordinated with the president and issued instructions to various agencies." [16]

—KAREN HUGHES

Groupie:
The U.S. has just been attacked and she's like totally happy with the way things have been handled—and isn't Dickie just dreamy?

Gatekeeper:
Everything goes through Cheney now, so George can lead a balanced life—Dick even gets first dibs on the cronies.

Mr. Peabody:
George Bush, the least informed person in the government was giving instructions to agencies? Don't make Dick laugh—he has a bad lip sprain.

❖ ❖ ❖

Move Along...Nothing To See Here

Hughes: Government Functioning Well
Brownie on vacation

"I was watching as the government functioned quite well: the calm, decision making I was witnessing there in the emergency center was far from the chaos I had imagined while listening to the news reports at home." [17]

—KAREN HUGHES

❖ ❖ ❖

The Mentor

Bush Takes Vice President Under His Wing
Delegates Commander-in-Chief role to apprentice Cheney to keep VP's confidence up

"You're doing great. I'll stay in touch with you." [18]

—George Bush to Cheney

A:

Cheney's the vice president; he attends funerals, chairs secret meetings and hobnobs with Kenny Boy.

B:

Bush, like the VP is also a pretentious condescending jackass, even if it is only Cheney being patronized.

2:50 PM

Air Force One lands at Offutt Air Force Base in Nebraska. It is very close to the geographical center of the continental United States, but if Bush wants to be extra far from all coastal areas, he should hole up in North Dakota the next time he runs away—the very middle, the donut hole of the North American land mass. Two air force bases—no waiting.

2:58 PM

Get Yosemite Sam On The Talky Box

**President Uses Old-Timey
Western Slang Term To Describe Terrorist**
Everyone assumes it to mean something uncomplimentary—only qualified interpreter died in 1952 at age 116

"At one point, he said he didn't want any tinhorn terrorist keeping him out of Washington." [19]

—Ari Fleischer

Folksy Festus:
When Bush catches up to them there terrorist fellers, he'll be all over them like ugly on an ape. He'll pound knots on their noggins faster'n they can rub 'em.

"If it's meant to be, it's going to happen. And therefore there's no need to try to hide from a terrorist." [20]

—GEORGE BUSH, EXPLAINING HIS "POST 9/11" HIDING PHILOSOPHY

3:10 PM

President Bush arrives at the Offutt Air Base Command Center and descends deep into the earth's crust—does a routine check for oil deposits.

3:30 PM

Live on ABC:

"He disappeared down the rabbit hole, Peter." [21]

—ANN COMPTON TO PETER JENNINGS

Where's Waldo?

Bush: People Want To Know Where Their President Is
Most had their money on Saskatoon or Cancun—43 percent didn't know he WAS president

"The American people want to know where their dang president is." [22]

—GEORGE BUSH

Cat got your tongue?

So what's the problem? Just craft another speech like the "git them folks" masterpiece at the school and flat out tell the adoring masses, "I'm in a very deep hole—and the décor is simply atrocious."

Holy Manliness, Batman

No Wrist Slapping This Time

And no noogies or wedgies either—not after the fiasco at Ashcroft's "contraband" pool party

> *"We're not going to have any slap-on-the-wrist crap this time."* [23]

> —GEORGE BUSH

Sweet dreams:

This time? Bush did not explode, swat or water board anyone during his time in office to that point—but, he did have a slap fight with that smartass waiter at the Red Lobster in Manchester, NH in 2000. He lost, but that could count. All you can eat, my ass.

Puberty

Bush:
Terrorists Prey On Weak Governments And People

And occasionally on rugged masculine types like me, said president

> *"I had time to think and a couple of thoughts emerged. One was that you're guilty, if you harbor a terrorist, because I knew these terrorists like al-Qaeda liked to prey on weak government and weak people."* [24]

> —GEORGE BUSH

Déjà vu:
The Taliban was given the same ultimatum by the United States a few years ago, but good original thinking. Everything is new if you never read anything.

Holy Harken, he's one of them savant fellers!
Several hours ago, the president couldn't go to the little boy's room without help and now he's developing the Bush Doctrine between solving Sunday New York Times crossword puzzles—in ink.

We'll Just Wait Until The Evildoers Stay At A Holiday Inn... Then "POW!"

"When I take action, I'm not going to fire a $2 million missile at a $10 empty tent and hit a camel in the butt. It's going to be decisive." [25]

—GEORGE BUSH,
AT SOME POINT BEFORE 9/11,
EVIDENTLY ANTICIPATING THAT A
CAMEL WOULD BE INVOLVED WHEN HE
GOT TOUGH, AS QUOTED IN THE
"THE LEADERSHIP GENIUS OF GEORGE
W. BUSH" BY CAROLYN B. THOMPSON
AND JAMES W. WARE

❖ ❖ ❖

Masculine Makeover

Enemies Won't Like Bush As President
He's their honey now—but wait until you see him in shoulder pads

"When we find out who did this, they are not going to like me as president. Somebody is going to pay." [26]

—GEORGE BUSH

Careful now:
You're giving Wolfowitz the vapors.

❖ ❖ ❖

"Goddamn whoever did this. Goddamn them." [27]

—GEORGE BUSH

4:00 PM

The National Security Council meets. Decide they should get together more often.

Break Out The Velveeta...
He's Comin' Home

Hughes: President Carried Us Through Crisis
Except for the dead people I mean—and the maimed

> *"He practically came through the television screen an hour or so later as he opened the meeting: 'We are war against terror, and from this day forward, this is the New Priority of our administration,' the president told his senior team, assembled at the White House, the Defense Department and the State Department. It was reassuring to see him: he looked calm, confident, in charge. President Bush was carrying us through this crisis, lifting us all through his sheer will and strength of personality. At the end of the meeting, although the Secret Service and others had warned against it, he brooked no more discussion: 'Get ready for me; I'm coming home,' he said."* [28]

> —KAREN HUGHES

Hmmm:
The NEW priority is to protect the country from attack?

The wind beneath our wings:
As soon as these pesky attacks are over, we'll have some forceful meetings by golly—and George will show everyone his new steely eye look. It's very impressive—almost like the one he made after Barney took a crap on the sports watchin' couch—but with just a touch of wistfulness.

Mr. Personality:
"Well Marge, I know the president was a cowardly buffoon during the attacks, but doesn't he have a nice way about him? Let's call him up and see if he wants to go fishing with us next weekend."

Erect a statue already:
Hours after the FAA declared the American skies clear; the noble president boldly decides to come back to D.C.

*"We're gonna get those bastards.
No thug is gonna bring our country down."* [29]

—GEORGE BUSH

Ain't Gonna Start Reading Stuff Now

Bush Didn't Need Legal Briefs
Just a fresh pair of regular briefs

> *"I can remember sitting right here in this office [on Air Force One] thinking about the consequences of what had taken place and realizing it was the defining moment in the history of the United States. I didn't need any legal briefs, I didn't need any consultations, I knew we were at war."* [30]

—GEORGE BUSH

Pre-Law:
He don't need no stinkin' legal briefs. Bush is a common sensical man of the people, don't ya see?

Childlike:
Bush boasts about the least bit of brain activity.

Payback time:
Evidently, Bush is still steamed about getting turned down for law school, forcing him to go to go to his fallback grad school…Harvard. Look who's president now—not one of you smarty pants legal brief guys with an adorable little leather suitcase, that's for sure.

Al K. Duh

CIA Director Believes Al Qaeda
Responsible For Attacks
Name sounds strangely familiar to president. "Did I borrow money from him, once?"

> *Mr. Bush had a question for CIA Director George Tenet. "George Tenet was just asked, 'Who do you think did this to us?,'" recalls Rice. "He said, 'Sir, I believe its al Qaeda. We're doing the assessment but it looks like, it feels like, it smells like al Qaeda.'"* [31]

—CONDI RICE

Quack:
It's a big fat smelly noisy Mallard, but we didn't think it would land in our lo-cal Cream of Ostrich soup.

❖ ❖ ❖

Secretary Of Agriculture

Snake Ranchers Beware Declares Bush
Lizard, salamander and toady farmers better watch their step, too

> *"These guys are like rattlesnakes. They'll go back in their hole. Not only will we strike the hole, we'll strike the rancher."* [32]

—GEORGE BUSH, EXPLAINING HIS STRATEGY ON SOMETHING

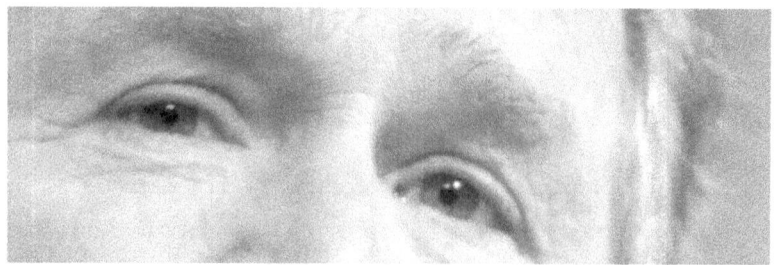

G-G-G-Georgie And The Jets

F-16's Protect President
Maybe these planes could be used in the future to defend other people in the country, thinks Bush

> *Bush, however, says he wasn't worried about the safety of the people on this aircraft, or for his own safety: "I looked out the airplane and saw two F-16s on each wing. It was going to have to be a pretty good pilot to get us."* [33]

—GEORGE BUSH ON 60 MINUTES II

Diva:
George gets four fighter planes—more than were initially sent to protect New York and Washington, D.C.

Supply side defense:
It would take a pretty good pilot to get to the World Trade Center, too—if one F-16 could have been spared to guard the country's largest city.

Yep, We Hit the Jackpot Alright

> *"To the extent that one is ever able to see the hand of God in history—and since biblical times, one has never been given the certitude in this regard—I believe that either divine intervention or good luck on the magnitude of a lottery win explains George W. Bush's rise to the position of president."* [34]
> —DENNIS PRAGER

CHAPTER ELEVEN

The Return
Of The Road Warrior

"Anyway, it was an interesting day."
—GEORGE BUSH

Bush was feeling pretty sassy after his death defying trip to the heartland. Air Force One landed at Andrews Air Force Base at 6:34 pm and Bush took the Marine One helicopter back to the White House and defiantly insisted on landing on the South Lawn as if the area were suddenly a terrorist stronghold. He tells a few lies to the American people before defiantly retiring to his own bed. He probably got up in the middle of the night and defiantly used the bathroom, too.

I Shall Return...Sevenish

Commander-in-Chief Lands On South Lawn
People rejoice—spontaneously meet town-hall style

> *"I'm landing on the South Lawn in Marine One. People want to see me land on the South Lawn at the White House and go into the Oval Office, okay?"* [1]

—GEORGE BUSH

It might be true:
It's conceivable that several people in the country were thinking, "Boy, I hope the president lands on the South Lawn. That'll show the terrorists who isn't hardly scared to travel with heavy military protection."

Mini courage:
Break it up folks. That was the president's brave moment for the day. He'll be kicking asses and taking names again in two, three days.

Green zone:
The groundskeeper is unimpressed though; "Pour some concrete already for chrissakes! Hey…you terrorists! Get off the grass!"

Turn The Other Cheek

They Took Their Best Shot Says President
Trying to stop them would have just been uncouth

> *"I don't remember thinking about whether or not the White House would have been obliterated. I think I might have thought they took their best shot, and now it was time for us to take our best shot."* [2]

—George Bush

Dueling banjos:
This isn't a game where we each take a turn. The passive one gets another thing mixed up with Hungry Hungry Hippos.

C'est La Vie:
That's the spirit! There's no shame in failing Mr. President—you'll be ready for anything after a few more years of training.

Impervious:
Remember the humans? The White House is just a building; but there were people inside.

8:30 PM

Not Under Oath
Only Technically A Liar, Not Legally

Bush Speaks To Nation
Uses photographic imagination to recall days events

> *"Immediately following the first attack, I implemented our*
> *government's emergency response plans. Our military is powerful,*
> *and it's prepared. Our emergency teams are working in New York City*
> *and Washington, D.C. to help with local rescue efforts. Our*
> *first priority is to get help to those who have been injured, and to*
> *take every precaution to protect our citizens at home and around*
> *the world from further attacks. The functions of our government*
> *continue without interruption. Federal agencies in Washington*
> *which had to be evacuated today are reopening for essential personnel*
> *tonight, and will be open for business tomorrow."*

> —GEORGE BUSH

Lie:
Bush didn't implement emergency response plans immediately or at any
other time.

Lie:
The Commander-in-Chief didn't have the military prepared to protect
people on this continent.

Lie:
Bush's first priority should have been to protect the country from further
attacks, but it wasn't. The Commander-in-Chief sat through a photo-op,
made a TV appearance and vamoosed to Louisiana and Nebraska before
giving a thought to his responsibilities.

Let them eat jet fuel:
Why weren't the people in the Pentagon warned of hijacked airliners headed
towards Washington, D.C.? Why hustle Cheney to an underground rat
hole and leave most others at their desks?

Pampered

9/11 Heck Of A Day—
President Sleeps In Own Bed
Couldn't find favorite jammies right away—Secret Service brings in an extra detail for search

> *"Oh no, we're not. I'm really tired. I've had a heck of a day and I'm going to sleep in my own bed."* [3]

—George Bush, refusing to sleep in a White House bunker on 9/11
"George and Laura"

Itty bitty bravery:
Sleeping in the lightly guarded White House—oh my! A person might think there would be plenty of 9/11 stories of courage to tell about the president, but this one made the cut in Mr. Andersen's book.

Blisters on phone finger:
It was a real bitch of a day for the president—compared to that Hilton woman. As people work non-stop to save those buried under the broken concrete and twisted steel, Bush whines about his tough times aboard a flying luxury hotel.

Let's Review

Bush returns to Washington, D.C. totally exhausted from playing "Cheney style" hide and seek—Dick tells the president to run and hide somewhere in the great plains, but nobody looks for him.

The Talking Points

CHAPTER TWELVE

Leadership
Postponed

"I believe results matter. Our leaders should be judged by results, not by entertaining personalities or clever sound bites."
—GEORGE BUSH "A CHARGE TO KEEP"

Since the president performed like he was on a blend of medical marijuana, OxyContin and NyQuil on the actual day of September 11th, the Bush administration simply moved the date for George Bush's 9/11 leadership to September 14th. It wasn't as hard as it sounds.

Seize the Wrong Day

President: America Knows Where I Stand
In the rubble—three days after an attack

> *"Three days after September 11th, I stood where Americans died, in the ruins of the Twin Towers. Workers in hard hats were shouting to me, 'Whatever it takes.' A fellow grabbed me by the arm and he said, 'Do not let me down.'* **Since that day,** *I wake up every morning thinking about how to better protect our country. I will never relent in defending America whatever it takes."*
>
> —GEORGE BUSH

Three days before 9/14:
Bush stood in his office on Air Force One as the plane zoomed west like a young Cheney from a draft notice. They were going so fast, he could hold his chocolate milk sideways without spilling.

Formica:
Since there was no substance on 9/11, all we get are snapshots of Bush standing in the ruins of his failure three days later. Be sure to order extra prints for the next fundraiser—and the folks.

Fond memories:
People were buried in Bush's favorite backdrop.

❖ ❖ ❖

A Good Diversion...Priceless

Hughes: Remember The Aftermath Leadership
It's all we have, so chew slowly and savor it—some ketchup couldn't hurt

> *"I can understand why some Democrats might not want the American people to remember the great leadership and strength the president and first lady Laura Bush brought to our country **in the aftermath** of that."* [1]

—Karen Hughes

Truth by omission:
Hughes, who looked directly into the camera on the afternoon of 9/11 and lied to the American people, can't bring herself to rave about the boss' leadership on "that" day. It's as close to candor as she's going to get.

❖ ❖ ❖

Liars Block

No Weakness On My Watch, Bush Says
Wimpiness, weaseliness, flaccidness—but not weakness

*"If America shows uncertainty or weakness during these troubled times, this world will drift toward tragedy. This is **not going to happen on my watch.**"*

—GEORGE BUSH

Head Injury?

9/11 happened on Bush's watch. He was uncertain and very weak. There's a big hole in the middle of Manhattan and thousands dead, but let's not talk about that.

Eagle Scout

Hughes: Bush Displayed Resolve And Leadership After 9/11

He's always prepared to take over after a crisis has passed

*"Senator McCain had gone too far in comparing Governor Bush to President Bill Clinton, and there was a hard glint in the governor's eye that gave voters a preview of the resolve and **leadership he would display after September 11:** Criticize me, but do not question my integrity."* [2]

—KAREN HUGHES "TEN MINUTES FROM NORMAL"

What a man:

We could have used the hard glint Bush on 9/11, instead of the dewy eyed, weak-kneed Bush.

Low quality:

Integrity? George? The Bush campaign savagely slimed and slandered the senator and his family during the 2000 presidential primaries—Bush was too cowardly to take responsibility.

Eye fetish?

"He leaned over and smiled, his (Bush's) blue eyes twinkling only about three inches from my (Hughes) face, and spoke in slow, exaggerated tones: "And you think a message meeting is more important than my speech to a historic joint session of Congress when our nation is at war?" [3]

—KAREN HUGHES "TEN MINUTES FROM NORMAL"

The President with the steely blues should have asked himself similar questions on 9/11:

"And you think a photo-op is more important than doing my job when our nation is under attack?"

"And you think writing a speech is more important than doing my job when our nation is under attack?"

"And you think a TV appearance is more important than doing my job when our nation is under attack?"

"And you think going to Nebraska is more important than doing my job when our nation is under attack?"

And He Rose Three Days Later

Bush: New Era Began On September 14, 2001
Triumphal pose struck on rubble of own country—political pay dirt

> *"None of us will ever forget that week when one era ended and another began. On September the 14th, 2001, I stood in the ruins of the Twin Towers. I'll never forget the day."*

—GEORGE BUSH

Date rape:
If there were any era's ending or starting, it was on 9/11, but nice sleazy try.

Calendar Girl

Hughes Doesn't Think In Terms Of Mistakes
Just bullhorns, rubble and puppy dog tails

Question:
You know the president well. He's been in the White House now for a thousand days. What do you think his biggest mistake has been and how has he learned from it?

Karen Hughes:
*"Tim, I don't know that I think in those terms. What I think in terms of is the extraordinary leadership that he provided our country in the **aftermath of September 11**. I remember standing with him in New York, the Friday after September 11 and watching him grab that bullhorn and speak to those rescue workers who couldn't hear him and he said, 'Well, I hear you, and the world hears you. And the people who knocked down those buildings are going to hear from all of us soon.' I think he is—you know, I'm his friend and I'm his advocate, and I don't look at him that way. What I look at is the extraordinary leadership he provided our country in a very, very difficult time."*[4]

Hey!
The president is proud of everything he did ON 9/11. Won't anyone acknowledge his steadfastness on that day—he nearly missed his lunch for crying out loud.

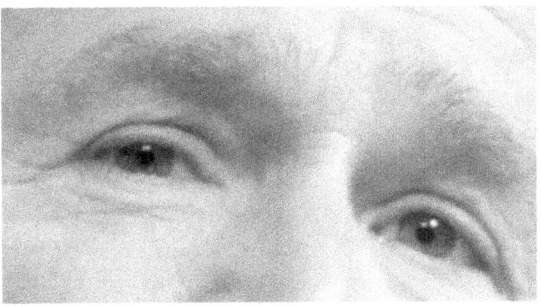

Pick A Talking Point...
Any Talking Point

Bush's Rubble Performance Convinces McCain
If standing on rubble three days after an attack isn't leadership, I don't
know what is

> *"I knew my confidence was well placed when I watched him stand on
> the rubble of the World Trade Center with his arm around a hero of
> September 11 and, in our moment of mourning and anger, strengthen
> our unity and our resolve by promising to right this terrible wrong
> and to stand up and fight for the values we hold dear."* [5]

—JOHN MCCAIN, 2004 REPUBLICAN CONVENTION

Very sad:
First they got Powell, and now McCain.

Politics before country:
McCain embraces a low quality
elitist weasel who doesn't have
enough character to carry the
Senator's shoes.

Sell-out:
Yep, Bush is a swell stander, but
the rubble symbolizes Bush's failure
and poor leadership on 9/11—not
a triumph.

South Carolina 2000 Presidential Primary—Bush Character In Action

Bush backers distributed handouts,
made telephone push polls and
started rumors that McCain had a
black baby by a hooker, his wife
was a drug addict, and that he was
unbalanced due to his years as a
prisoner of war in Viet Nam.

The Great Comforter
He's Like A Blanket, Only Thicker

**Bush Inspired Comfort And Pride
After Attacks Says VP**
Inspired Americans to fend for themselves during attacks

> *"In the weeks **following the terrorist attacks** on America, people in
> every part of the country, regardless of party, took great comfort and
> pride in the conduct and the character of our president. They saw a
> man calm in a crisis, comfortable with responsibility, and determined
> to do everything necessary to protect our people."* [6]

—DICK CHENEY

Dumb & dumber:
Cheney was supposed be keeping an eye on the kid and he had no clue on
9/11 either. These guys are the grownup's we heard so much about?

Groundhog:
Bush was calm alright; he didn't even come out of his hole until he
stopped trembling three days later.

Mulligan

President Vows To Protect America After 9/11
But only during regular business hours and one Saturday a month—
no Augusts

> *"I vowed to the American people **after that fateful day**
> of September the 11th that we would not rest nor tire until
> we're safe."* [7]

—GEORGE BUSH

Steadfast my ass:
Bush gave an oath on the day of his inauguration, but that vow didn't take. So…he simply moves the goal and reneges on the prior commitment. But by God, after that fateful day, he's really going to bear down and do his job. Not because it's in his job description, though—but just because he cares so darn much.

George W. Bush
January 20, 2001

"I do solemnly swear that I will faithfully execute the office of President of the United States, and will to the best of my ability, preserve, protect, and defend the Constitution of the United States."

❖ ❖ ❖

The Greatest Publicity Stunt Ever

September 14:
Defining Moment In American History Says Bush
9/11 is up there, too—but that's ancient history

"It was one of those defining moments in American history." [8]

—GEORGE BUSH

High on life:
Who knew that the deaths of thousands of people could be the high point in a president's term? Let's hope standing around during terrorist attacks doesn't catch on as a political technique.

❖ ❖ ❖

The Trump Card

September 14 Nearly As Important As 9/11
Bush ranks it just ahead of Civil War and Texas Air National Guard reunion

"Bush knew that September 11 was the day everyone would remember for eternity. But as far as he was concerned, September 14 was nearly as important." [9]

—BILL SAMMON

No kidding:
We would never hear the end of the bullhorn moment.

❖ ❖ ❖

Un-Standardized Testing

"America Now Awake"
Campaign Chairman Racicot Declares
Recommends that some of us stay alert while the others nap—like those funny little meerkat critters

*"There is no better place to celebrate President Bush's leadership and present his vision for the future than here in New York. In this city George W. Bush confronted one of the greatest tests of leadership ever to face a President. In this city **America finally awoke** to the realities of a world at war." [10]*

—MARC RACICOT, FORMER GOVERNOR OF MONTANA AND BUSH-CHENEY '04 CAMPAIGN CHAIRMAN AT 2004 REPUBLICAN CONVENTION

Nice try:
America is a country, not a conscious entity—the nation did not fall asleep.

Baywatch Bush:
"It wasn't me who fell asleep and those people drowned. It was America. It's society's fault, man."

Weasel words:
George Bush didn't confront anything in New York on 9/11. Cause, he was leavin' on a jet plane, didn't know when he'd be back again—oh babe he hated to go.

The Little General

President Extra Decisive Says Hughes
Usually only fairly decisive—less barking

> *"He has always been decisive; he was more so. He has always been focused; he was more focused than I have ever seen him. He's always in charge at meetings; now he was barking orders like a drill sergeant."* [11]

> —KAREN HUGHES

Swoon city:
Just imagine the adjectives if the boss wasn't an empty suit.

I'm Just A Gigolo

Thousands Of New Yorkers Dead And Wounded
Giuliani thankful for George Bush

> *"President Bush's response in keeping us unified and in turning the ship of state around from being solely on defense against terrorism to being on offense as well and for his holding us together. For that and then his determined effort to defeat global terrorism, no matter what happens in this election, President George W. Bush already has earned a place in our history as a great American President."* [12]

> —RUDOLPH GIULIANI AT 2004 REPUBLICAN CONVENTION

Tool:
George Bush failed to keep New Yorkers safe. He choked and ran away. That doesn't bother Rudy, though.

Tell Us About
The Boy From New York City

George W. Bush Calls Evil By It's Name
Mookie

> *"We all remember that terrible morning when, in the space of just 102 minutes, more Americans were killed than we lost at Pearl Harbor. We remember the President who* **came to New York City** *and pledged that the terrorists would soon hear from all of us. George W. Bush saw this country through grief and tragedy, he has acted with patience, and calm, and a moral seriousness that calls evil by its name."* [13]

—Vice President Dick Cheney

New York City!
President Bush couldn't get far enough away from the Big Apple. He was already in Florida and thought that was too close.

Only 102 minutes?
The same length of Keanu Reeves' movie "Hardball." It wasn't that short.

Slight difference:
At Pearl Harbor we fought back. On 9/11, the calm and patient Commander-in-Chief took the wait and see approach—in a hole.

Spiro on acid trip:
Moral indeed. Bush had a moral obligation to use his power to defend the people of this country. He didn't.

Shy

Bush Finally Decisive, Recalls Hughes
No opportunities to show off decisive leadership skills during the attacks

> *"America was **finally seeing** the decisive leader those of us who worked for him knew so well."* [14]

—Karen Hughes, talking about Bush on 9/14

Super leak:

Hughes, talking about Bush on the 14th, admits the president hadn't shown any previous decisive leadership to America—at least not the visible type.

It's Haaard Work!

Since 9/11:
President Ponders Protection Of Country

Bush used to think about…actually he was pretty much a blank slate

> ***"Ever since that day,*** *I wake up every morning trying to figure out how to better protect our country."* [15]

—George Bush

Brain cramp:

Just don't do any ciphering before breakfast—and probably lunch.

Pre 9/11:

zzzzzzzzzzz$$$$$$$ZZZZZ???????zzzzzzzzzzz

Dormant Leadership

Hughes: 9/11 Brought Out The Best In Bush

Well, that makes it all worthwhile

> *"I like to say you don't acquire the kind of qualities of character and leadership. You either—you know, you've developed them over a lifetime or you haven't. So you don't become someone different when you respond to something. I think this brought out the best in him. I like to say he's more so. He's a—he's always been disciplined; he's more so. He's always been focused; he's more so. He's always been, you know, absolutely engaged in leading our team; and he's more so. He clearly*

*has a mission and he knows that the rest of his presidency will be
focused on securing our homeland, going after those who threaten our
security, and fighting this war against terror. And he knows that. And
he knows it's his responsibility. And as long as he's president, that will
be his first thought every morning and his last thought every night."* [16]

—KAREN HUGHES

Slow learner:
It took Bush a whole "lifetime" to acquire the miniscule leadership skills he
displayed on 9/11? How long did it take before he could say, "oh, and I'll
need all of the land around my new stadium, too"?

Stuck in first gear:
Disciplined, focused, engaged—Bush was all that before 9/11, but just
short of a full dose. But after a shot of "rubble 'roids" he's fully loaded
with character, clarity and a sense of responsibility—plus shrunken testicles.

Isn't that poetic:
First thought in morning, last at night. Gag me.

Better late:
Conveniently, the president's duties are the same as they were before 9/11, but
now his eyeballs are in focus, so everything should be OK from here on out.

Over The Line

Rudy Giuliani is one of few national figures willing to say the president
did a good job on the actual day of 9/11. It's a lie, but music to the ears
of George Bush.

Condi Rice wriggles out of telling an outright lie, but she still infers that
the boss performed well.

Rumsfeld was barely conscious on 9/11, but he has some very fond
recollections of the president.

I Just Called To Say I Love You

Bush Terrific Leader Claims Giuliani

He sat there like a champ—you could have set a glass of champagne on his head

> *"So I can't express to you how appreciative we are of your acting so swiftly. And, also, on that terrible day when our city was being attacked, you were in immediate communication with us, Mr. President, and helped to secure the city. And the work you've done for us, we all eternally appreciate. You've been a terrific leader and we're taking direction from you, and we're following your example. You've done a terrific job, Mr. President."* [17]

—RUDOLPH GIULIANI

Dial M for moron:

The meathead thought the attacks were over and was calling the mayor to offer financial assistance for the victims and the cleanup effort. Doesn't count. Bush didn't do anything to secure the city.

Royal suck up:

Thousands of New York citizens are dead. Well, that's just terrific.

Role model:

Let that be lesson to the kids—do a crappy job and Mayor Giuliani will shower you with praise. Don't count on the mayor of New Orleans, though—he gets pretty cranky when his people die.

Quid Pro Quo

Rice Won't Forget Leadership Of President

As long as she stays Secretary of State and gets all of the coupons from the Sunday paper

"And as an officer of government on duty that day, I will never forget the sorrow and the anger that I felt, nor will I forget the courage and resilience of the American people, nor the leadership of the president that day." [18]

—Condi Rice

Weasel words:
Rice might not forget the leadership of the president, but she didn't say it was good.

Kiss ass:
It gets a little sickening—but there's a promotion on the line.

You Look Very Nice Today Mrs. Cleaver

President Commanding and Impressive In Person Says Rumsfeld
The lighting at the Omaha underground hideout really brought out the color of his eyes on the video monitors

"As one of those working with him on his national security team, I can report that throughout the crisis, the president has been as commanding and impressive in person as he has been in his public addresses." [19]

—Donald Rumsfeld September 12, 2001

Suck it up:
Come on Don—if you ever want to legally blow anything up again, you have to say it. Sehr gut! Now cluck like a chicken. Oh, very funny, Rumsfeld—hardy har har—I meant like the bird, not like the president.

"There are 400 neatly marked graves somewhere in Sicily all because one man went to sleep on his job—but they were German graves for we caught the bastard asleep before his officers did."
—GENERAL GEORGE PATTON

CHAPTER THIRTEEN

Brave
New World

*"See, in my line of work you got to keep repeating things
over and over and over again for the truth to sink in,
to kind of catapult the propaganda."*
—GEORGE W. BUSH

*"Those who have spent their entire life in politics
often become spin artists rather than thinkers.
They lose attention span."*
—RUDOLPH GIULIANI "LEADERSHIP"

It would be embarrassing and moronic if the threat from al Qaeda existed before 9/11 and the president had done nothing to defend the country, so he simply declares everything to be brand spanking new. The enemy, the type of war—you name it, and unbeknownst to most Americans, the responsibility for defense is now a **new** chore for the government. You can't expect George to defend against an enemy that didn't exist until they appeared out of thin air on 9/11, especially when it wasn't even his job. And if there was a threat, and Bush is not saying there was, it's all our faults for not paying closer attention.

New Kind Of War

Morning After Pill

Bush Understands
Dozens of former classmates drop dead—coffins declared off-limits to media

"It's a new kind of war. And I understand it's a new kind of war." [1]

—GEORGE BUSH

Parse farce:
Find the enemy and kill them.
Yeah, that's new.

Trusted Advisor Keeps Huge Secret From President

"The terrorist threat to our nation did not emerge on September 11, 2001. Long before that day, radical, freedom-hating terrorists declared war on America and on the civilized world." [2]

—CONDI RICE

❖ ❖ ❖

Guns, Bombs, Sand... But No Beachheads

Baby Boomers Used To Quagmire In Viet Nam
Some more than others

"I understand this is an unconventional war. It's a different kind of war. It's not the kind of war that we're used to in America. The Greatest Generation was used to storming beachheads. Baby boomers such as myself, were used to getting caught in a quagmire of Vietnam where politics made decisions more than the military sometimes. Generation X was able to watch technology right in front of their TV screens—you know, burrow into concrete bunkers in Iraq and blow them up. This is a different kind of war that requires a different type of approach and a different type of mentality." [3]

—GEORGE BUSH

Gibberish:
Terrorists said they were going to attack America and then did. What do beachheads, Generation X and burrowing have to do with a crater in Manhattan and a big hole in the Pentagon?

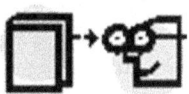

No...Not Really That New

"According to the State Department, there were 230 terrorist incidents between January 1968 and September 11, 2001 in which a total of almost 1,000 Americans were killed." [4]

—DONALD RUMSFELD

❖ ❖ ❖

Previous Generations
A Bunch Of Map Marking Sissies

This War Most Dangerous Says Rove
WWII was a joke compared to fighting the cave lurkers and shadow hiders

"And the chopper was very quiet, and the President was on the left-hand side of the chopper. And he said, 'Take a close look. You are looking at the face of war in the 21st century,' and I thought about that later because, right from the beginning, he knew it was a different

kind of war. This was not one that was fought like our parents or grandparents fought or observed with, you know, a map on the front page of your newspaper and you could mark…and the armies that cross France or tout up how many divisions each one had or how many tanks, that this was a much more dangerous and difficult kind of a war fought against an enemy who hides in shadows and lurks in caves. It was clear right from the beginning that to him, this was that kind of war." [5]

—KARL ROVE,
DESCRIBING HOW HIS IMAGINATION WAS TRIGGERED BY THE PRESIDENT
DURING THE 9/11 RIDE TO THE WHITE HOUSE ON MARINE ONE

OK, we get it:
New kind of war, Bush figured it out—good for him.

Subtle:
The Nazi's were way more sporting with their non-lurking Panzer divisions—and those noisy u-boats.

Cockroach:
Yes Karl, during the Big One, the greatest generation families used to sit at the kitchen table after dinner with multi-colored highlighters and track military movements on the daily paper. Everyone has boxes of that crap in their attic—right by the ant farm.

They Started Without Us… Stupid Cheaters

"The terrorists were at war with us, but we were not yet at war with them."

—CONDI RICE,
9/11 COMMISSION REPORT

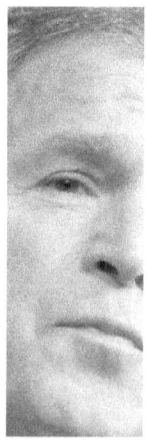

Defaced

Faceless Cowards Attack World's Mightiest Nation
See their photos in your local newspaper

"It's the new war. It's the faceless coward that attacks."

—GEORGE BUSH

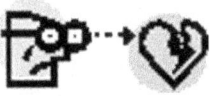

Clinton's Old War

"But the big failure of the Clinton administration was not only not in getting bin Laden, it was not in making the air system safe. We had lots of crashes, lots of hijackings. We had the TWA 800 flight that people thought as terrorism. We knew the terrorists were targeting airplanes." [6]

—DICK MORRIS, TRYING TO HELP GEORGE BUSH'S CASE, I GUESS.

❖ ❖ ❖

Rovian Rhapsody

Rove: Easier To Fight Nation States
Especially ones with no airplanes or those big boats

"... it's a different kind of war. We are facing a threat that we've never faced before, which is this threat of trans-national global terrorism. Before, we've always faced nation states, and facing a nation state is actually in a way better because there are constraints on a national leadership. If you are a country and you attack the United States, you got to worry about being attacked in return. If you are a terrorist network, you are simply using a country as a sanctuary and you don't

care about it as long as you've got another place to go to. So it makes global terrorism a different kind of a threat, and as a result makes it difficult to compare it to other kinds of conflicts which we've been. It is a conflict. It is a war. It is a particularly dangerous kind of war because the adversary we face has fewer constraints." [7]

—KARL ROVE

Rove rubbish:
Evidently, the object is to change the subject and try to bore the interviewer to death.

Bogosity:
Oh, how right you are, oh porcine purveyor of phony tales. Hitler was really constrained; he wouldn't have used the bomb if the Germans had developed it first. And the Japanese were so polite—and don't get me started on what swell guys the Viet Cong were. Who wouldn't enjoy a year in the jungle with those dudes—George really missed out on the fun in southeast Asia.

From The Old Terrorism To The New: The First World Trade Center Bombing

—9/11 COMMISSION REPORT HEADING

At 18 minutes after Noon on February 26, 1993, a huge bomb went off beneath the two towers of the World Trade Center.

Lie:
Global terrorism new? The only place free of terrorist cells before 9/11 was the North Pole.

Tour Guide

Pentagon On Fire
Bush nostalgic for the peaceful terrorist sit-ins of the 20th century

"The mightiest building in the world is on fire. That's the twenty-first-century war you've just witnessed."

—GEORGE BUSH, AS HIS HELICOPTER PASSES THE PENTAGON
ON THE WAY BACK TO THE WHITE HOUSE ON 9/11.

Say, this IS new:
In the 20th century, we didn't let suicide planes fly around for hours before hitting the Pentagon.

The New War In The 1980's... Those Were The Good New Days

President Reagan's second secretary of state, George Shultz, advocated active U.S. efforts to combat terrorism, often recommending the use of military force.

—9/11 COMMISSION REPORT

❖ ❖ ❖

Rinse...Repeat

Hughes:
This Enemy Sends Young Men Out To Kill
And they aren't very polite about it, either

"I remember the first week after September 11th, he—every morning when I saw him, he kept telling me we've got to educate the America people about what a dif—the different nature of this enemy, the different kind of war that this is. He drove that into all of our heads every day for weeks. Because it really is different. It's different from, you know, moving armies or conquering territory. It's a—it's really a threat from a faceless enemy who hides and sends other—you know, as he says, sends young men out to kill on behalf of people who hide in caves. So it's very different. And I have been very impressed by the

patience that the American people have shown, by their understanding of the threat. Because it is different. It's different than any threat we've ever faced, and it's a very insidious, long-lasting threat to our country." [8]

—KAREN HUGHES

Echo:
Is it different? Karen, can you repeat the part about being different a few more times, please?

Elementary:
Education? Yes, that's the solution. The American people were ignorant about the hiding cave people. There was no way to defend against the faceless hordes with such a stupid electorate. We should all be ashamed.

Support the troops:
Well, Karen's got a valid point there. No leader has ever sent young men and women out to kill, and watched the mayhem from a safe distance.

Hiders In The Homeland— 2000 AD

Richard Clarke wrote Samuel Berger on January 11, 2000, that the CIA, the FBI, Justice, and the NSC staff had come to two main conclusions. First, U.S. disruption efforts thus far had "not put too much of a dent" in bin Ladin's network. If the United States wanted to "roll back" the threat, disruption would have to proceed at "a markedly different tempo." Second, "sleeper cells" and "a variety of terrorist groups" had turned up at home.

—9/11 COMMISSION REPORT

The Education President

Al Qaeda In 60 Countries Says Bush
Only in 59 countries before 9/11, but now in Antarctica, too—that tears it!

> *"This is a different war from any our nation has ever faced, a war on many fronts, against terrorists who operate in more than 60 different countries. And this is a war that must be fought not only overseas, but also here at home."* [9]

—GEORGE BUSH

Goober:
Oh, poor silly stupid naive George. This is old news to everybody but you.

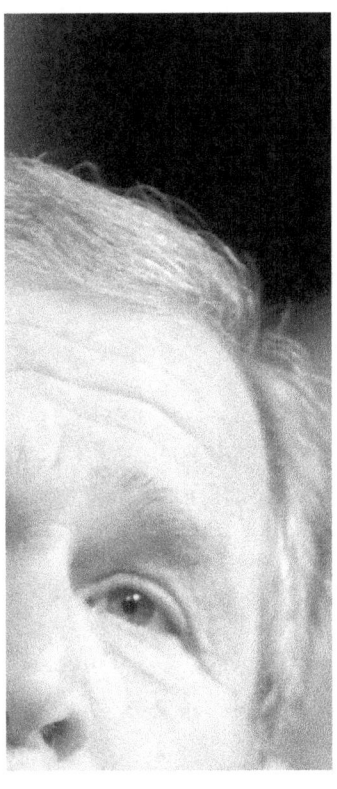

1993 Attack Began New War According To "Bush Country" Author

"Indeed, the country would have been better off if Clinton and Gore had been far less humble and far more sweeping in their assertion of American power—if they had seen that the 1993 attack on the World Trade Center, the 1998 attacks on U.S. embassies in Africa, and the 2000 attack on the USS Cole were the initial shots in the war on terror that escalated into unprecedented carnage on September 11." [10]

—JOHN PODHORETZ,
"BUSH COUNTRY: HOW DUBYA
BECAME A GREAT PRESIDENT WHILE
DRIVING LIBERALS INSANE"

A Secret War

In The Dark

Senator:
We Were At War, But Nobody Would Tell Us
Miller has a super low security clearance—too many duels in the cloakroom

> *"Even before 9/11 we were at war, but nobody would tell us we were at war. It was kind of kept from us."* [11]

—ZELL MILLER

Hell Zell:
Why have you forsaken us? Could you not get a secret message out to us about the secret war—perhaps using an incomprehensible folksy analogy about snakes under the porch or something?

Tell Zell:
At least you could have mentioned it to Bush. He would have known what to do.

A Different Country

Happy, Innocent And Weak...
It Was So Freakin Wonderful

We're A Different Country, Says Bush
Less people, fewer tall buildings—and political capital up to my eyeballs

> *"We are a different country than we were on September the 10th— sadder and less innocent; stronger and more united; and in the face of ongoing threats, determined and courageous."* [12]

—GEORGE BUSH

September 10:
In the jungle, the mighty jungle, the lion sleeps…

Party Like It's 1999

Washington and New York were identified as possible terrorist targets during the New Year's millennium celebrations. [13]

New Responsibilities

Terrorists On Double Secret Probation Until Now

Government Now Responsible For Defense
That's just crazy enough to work—we'll need more bombs, though

> *"We've added a new era, and this new era requires new responsibilities, both for the government and for our people."* [14]

—GEORGE BUSH

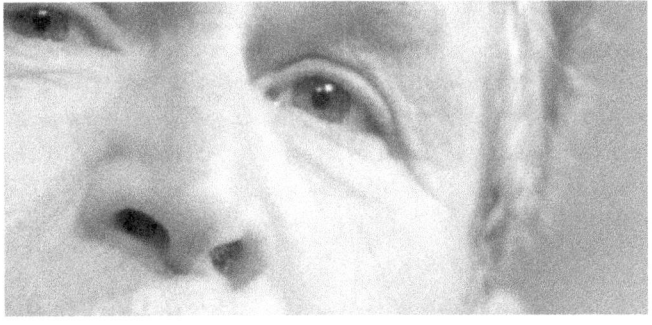

Not mandatory:
True patriots will plaster at least a dozen, "Don't support the terrorists" bumper stickers on their car to fight the scourge. The sacrifice of the paint job will not be in vain. Tax cuts are in the mail.

D'oh! Government Already Responsible For Defense Says Bush In 1999 Tell All Book

"*The federal government has some compelling purposes: to defend our homeland, to help keep peace in the world, to help secure the retirement and health needs of our senior citizens, and to help our society confront human suffering.*"

—GEORGE BUSH "A CHARGE TO KEEP"

❖ ❖ ❖

Try Squinting

Administration Now Focused On Need For Homeland Defense

Maybe we could create a cabinet position—like Secretary of Defense

"*But from January through Tuesday, we have focused on the new world we live in, on the need for homeland defense, on the need to reorder the priorities in the Department of Defense, and in the U.S. government. And the need to recognize that we have to think anew about the world we're in.*"[15]

—DONALD RUMSFELD

Zany office mix-up:
You guys have been focused since January? Are you sure Don, because the president thinks the new world just popped up in September?

He Didn't Say "Continental" United States, Though

"In 1998, Usama bin Laden publicly declared war on the United States."

—From 12/2000 Richard Clarke Paper "Strategy for Eliminating the Threat from the Jihadist Networks of al Qida: Status and Prospects." Clarke gave his plan to Condi Rice.

❖ ❖ ❖

Factual Relativism

Bush:
New Responsibilities For Government
Not sure who was handling that stuff before—it was probably that jerk Kevin

"After September the 11th, our government assumed new responsibilities to strengthen security at home and track down our enemies abroad." [16]

—George Bush

Karma:
What a coincidence. There was also a terrorist attack on September the 11th. Well, if the government wasn't responsible for security until after the 11th, it's hardly fair to criticize anyone in charge of that fine institution for not defending against an assault on the very day before the administration took charge of that little chore.

Seven Months Until 9/11

"Osama bin Laden and his global network of lieutenants and associates remain the most immediate and serious threat. As we have increased security around government and military facilities, terrorists are seeking out 'softer' targets that provide opportunities for mass casualties." [17]

—CIA DIRECTOR GEORGE TENET
BEFORE THE SENATE SELECT
COMMITTEE ON INTELLIGENCE
FEBRUARY 7, 2001

A Different World

Combat Pay Increase

Presidential Responsibilities Change
Bush still peace president on 9/11—lots of red tape in going directly from pussy president to war president

> *"The world changed for me on September 11, to the point every threat then had to be reexamined. My presidency changed. I went from a peace president to a war president."* [18]

—GEORGE BUSH

Red faced:
On 9/11, Bush thought there was a three-day waiting period (got mixed up with dang rules for buying one of those Dirty Harry guns) before he would officially become a war president and could take subsequent "warlike actions" on the offending party or "attacker." He feels a little sheepish about it, but the president now completely understands that "defensive measures" can be taken immediately against "attackers," even while an attack is in progress.

President Aware Of Terrorism Threat On Inauguration Day

It was only a couple decades old in January, so Bush still technically in the clear

"The President, on January 20th, was aware, that that is the new type of threat America faces from international terrorism." [19]

—ARI FLEISCHER

❖ ❖ ❖

Mom, Al Qaeda Is Coloring Outside The Lines

Rumsfeld Misses Safe Wars Of Yore
The Nerf shoulder fired missile is now only a relic of more civilized times

"It's also recognition that the world has changed; that we can no longer count on future wars being waged safely in their regions of origin." [20]

—DONALD RUMSFELD

Oh Don:
Will your elegant bullshit ever cease to amaze?

Big Time Delegation

American People Accept New Responsibility
Most citizens still not getting daily intelligence briefs, the
lifetime bennies—or piggyback rides over puddles

> *"I think the American people do understand that after September 11th,
> that we're facing a different world. And they accept that responsibility."* [21]

—GEORGE BUSH

And none too soon:
Pass out the Stingers and call a
moratorium on ammo smaller than
50 caliber.

New policy:
All citizens will now get a turn at
being president—one hour each.
The Secret Service is freaking out.

March 2000

According to U.S. intelligence,
information indicates that bin
Laden's organization might attack
places like the Statue of Liberty,
skyscrapers, ports, airports and
nuclear power plants. [22]

You Are Getting Sleepy

Rice Can't Remember World Before 9/11
Except not telling president about al Qaeda cells in the U.S.—she doesn't
remember that very clearly

> *"The world has changed so much that it is hard remember what our
> lives were like before that day."* [23]

—CONDI RICE

Pleasantville:
Those were the days—when a National Security Advisor could pull on a pair of Dockers, relax and BS with the guys over a glass of white zinfandel and a Cuban Montecristo—and the thought of terrorism was just a glimmer in the fat guy's creepy right eye.

A New Enemy

They're Cousins, Identical Cousins

Al Qaeda Dramatically Different Than Al Qaeda
Dramatically different reasoning utilized to highlight dissimilarity

> *"Now I was in charge of helping the president communicate during a global war against a diffuse and dramatically different enemy to people both at home and across the globe, many of whom clearly didn't seem to like us very much."* [24]

—KAREN HUGHES

Reverse alias:
The al Qaeda gang has the same name as before they became dramatically different to avoid confusion in marketing campaigns, plus bin Laden saves a ton of money by not having to redo all of the stationery.

Al Qaeda With More Calories

Rumsfeld Announces The New Improved al Qaeda
Previous destruction by al Qaeda laughable—the Secretary scoffs derisively

> *"The nature of the war we are fighting today, and the adversary we face, is unlike anything our nation has faced before."* [25]

—DONALD RUMSFELD

There's really no comparison:
al Qaeda was a nasty bunch—good heavens, they even attacked a U.S. Navy ship in late 2000, but these al Qaeda guys are really mean bastards.

He Has Spoken

People Need To Know We Face A Different Enemy
Everything else is none of their beeswax

> *"The American people need to know that we are facing a different enemy than we have ever faced. Those are the President's words."*[26]

—Ari Fleischer

Also:
He says to tell you that he's still manly, even though he ran away like a little girl. Enemy different, George Bush the same—any questions, not you, Helen…anyone?

No Planes, Trains Or Submarines

Terrorists Have No Tarmac Or Ships
Except for the borders, it sounds like Iraq

> *"Well, as the President has indicated, this is a different type of enemy in the 21st century. The President said, this enemy is nameless; this enemy is faceless; this enemy has no specific borders. This enemy does not have airplanes sitting on tarmacs and it does not have ships that move from one port city to the next. It is a different kind of enemy."*[27]

—Ari Fleischer

Organ donors:
No faces? Well, that's simply disgusting. What exactly happened to the faces? Did the enemy have names and faces before 9/11, or is this a new thing? Are there any other body parts or means of identification they don't have? How about Y membership cards—do any of them have those? Laminated ones? Maybe their names are on the cards?

German chocolate:
No airplanes or ships? This is going to be a cakewalk.

Clear And Present Danger

"When it comes to terrorism, time is a luxury we don't have. Some are even now saying we should just go slow on this legislation. Well, Congress has a right to review this legislation to make sure the civil liberties of American citizens are not infringed, and I encourage them to do that. But they should not go slow. Terrorists do not go slow, my fellow Americans. Their agenda is death and destruction on their own time-table. And we need to make sure that we can do everything possible to stop them from succeeding."

—BILL CLINTON,
1995 AIR FORCE ACADEMY SPEECH

❖ ❖ ❖

Its News To Him

This Enemy Hides, Says Bush
As a child, president was also puzzled by "hide and seek"

"The American people need to know that we're facing a different enemy than we have ever faced. This enemy hides in shadows, and has no regard for human life. This is an enemy who preys on innocent and unsuspecting people, then runs for cover. But it won't be able to run for cover forever. This is an enemy that tries to hide. But it won't be able to hide forever." [28]

—GEORGE BUSH

Well, that's just perfect:
We distinctly ordered a non-hiding enemy with a high regard for human life and you bring us these hideous shadow hiders! Take them back right now—we're not paying for these!

New Security Environment

Makes The Black Plague Look Like A Case Of The Sniffles

Most Dangerous World Ever
Rumsfeld shocked and awed—but still dismissive and quite unbalanced

"But this much is certain: on September 11th, our world changed—and while it may be tempting to think that once this crisis has passed and our nation has healed, things can go back to the way they were—we cannot go back. The world of September 10th is past. We have entered a new security environment, arguably the most dangerous the world has known. And if we are to continue to live as free people, we cannot go back to thinking as we did on September 10th." [29]

—DONALD RUMSFELD

We who?
Who wants to go back? Are they nuts? Go back to before 9/11, when the terrorists were plotting, and Rummy and Dummy whiled away the hours sipping carbonated water with little parings of citrus fruit skins floating invitingly just below the surface? I don't think so.

Black kettle caller:
The old and wise Secretary of Defense Donald "I didn't know what hit the Pentagon, how should I know" Rumsfeld lectures the rest of us to face the so-called new environment.

New Reason

Another Version Of Diversion

Terrorists Being Fought Since 9/11 To Save Lives
Earlier fights were just for fun—some pride, mostly fun

> *"Since the terrible morning of September the 11th, 2001,*
> *we fought the terrorists across the Earth—not for pride,*
> *not for power, but because the lives of our citizens are at stake."*[30]

—GEORGE BUSH

Fashionably Late

Bush Administration Now Focused On Security
No more all-night strip bingo at Bennett's house for milk money—those days are over, people

> *"The nation must understand, this is now the focus of my*
> *administration. We will be very much engaged in domestic*
> *policy, of course. I look forward to working with Congress on*
> *a variety of issues. But now that war has been declared on us,*
> *we will lead the world to victory."*[31]

—GEORGE BUSH

Aww darn:
We were hoping the focus
would continue to be photo-ops,
fundraisers and vacations with
the cronies.

Not properly notarized:
Bin Laden declared war on the U.S.
years ago, but don't tell George—
it will only make him feel bad.
Then we'll end up in a whole martyr
scene. "Oh, it's all my fault, I
should have known about that
and done something. Lord knows
I've tried, but frankly, I'm just not
that bright." He's so hard on himself, which is commendable, but it
gets a little sickening.

Fighting Terrorism In 1999

*"As we work for peace, we must also
meet threats to our nation's security—
including increased dangers from out-
law nations and terrorism. We will
defend our security wherever we are
threatened, as we did this summer
when we struck at Osama bin Laden's
network of terror. The bombing of
our embassies in Kenya and Tanzania
reminds us again of the risks faced
every day by those who represent
America to the world."*

—BILL CLINTON, JANUARY 19, 1999
STATE OF THE UNION SPEECH

A New Dread

My Kingdom For An Expert

Frum: Few Dreaded 9/11 Type Attack
He asked around

> *"September 11 was a moment that had been dreaded by almost
> nobody except for a few terrorist experts."* [32]

—DAVID FRUM

Pointy head free zone:
Bush likes to keep an expert free environment. Those well read types with the fancy printed-up four year college degrees really piss him off, with their, "I know about this, I know about that." Who needs it? Goldie will do fine.

1985— Ronald Reagan Plagiarizes Bush Doctrine

Speaking to the American Bar Association in July 1985, the President characterized terrorism as "an act of war" and declared: "There can be no place on earth left where it is safe for these monsters to rest, to train, or practice their cruel and deadly skills. We must act together, or unilaterally, if necessary to ensure that terrorists have no sanctuary—anywhere.

—9/11 COMMISSION REPORT

New Battlefield

Untidy

Different Kind Of Conflict Says Rumsfeld
Adding sort of, somewhat—and maybe just a smidge

> *"We are, in a sense, seeing the definition of a new battlefield in the world, a 20th–21st century battlefield, and it is a different kind of conflict. It is something that is not unique to this century, to be sure, but it is—given our geography and given our circumstance, it is, in a major sense, new for this country."* [33]

—DONALD RUMSFELD

Under duress:
Rumsfeld recited that nonsense like he had a gun pointed at his head—perhaps a Lady Smith & Wesson, good for some afternoon varmint pinging or that well deserved night on the town with the other 6'2" women of the White House.

No Safe Harbor

During 1995 and 1996, President Clinton devoted considerable time to seeking cooperation from other nations in denying sanctuary to terrorists. He proposed significantly larger budgets for the FBI, with much of the increase designated for counterterrorism. For the CIA, he essentially stopped cutting allocations and supported requests for supplemental funds for counterterrorism.

—9/11 Commission Report

New Outlook

Nation Had The Giggles

Threats Not Taken Seriously By Bush Pre-9/11
No kidding

> *"After 9/11, we had to recognize that when we saw a threat, we must take it seriously before it comes to hurt us."*[34]

—George Bush

Bush league:
He's predictable. Bush took hurricane Rita very seriously after ignoring the killer storm Katrina. Apparently, he needs a practice crisis to get the bugs out of his response for each type of disaster.

Pentagon And WTC In Crosshairs

According to a 1995 report by Philippine police, a plot to use hijacked airliners to hit targets, including the CIA headquarters, the Pentagon and the World Trade Center was uncovered after they broke up a terrorist cell.[35]

Bus Stop

I Just Waited For Attacks Before 9/11 Says Bush
It was really quite tedious

> *"After September the 11th, our object in the war on terror is not to wait for the next attack and respond, but to prevent attacks by taking the fight to the enemy."*[36]

—GEORGE BUSH

Single minded:
And defense, too? Next time, we can defend ourselves, right? Or is that still out?

President Reagan Deals With The New War

After the killing of the marines in Beirut, President Reagan signed National Security Directive 138, calling for a "shift…from passive to active defense measures" and reprogramming or adding new resources to effect the shift. It directed the State Department "to intensify efforts to achieve cooperation of other governments" and the CIA to "intensify use of liaison and other intelligence capabilities and also to develop plans and capability to preempt groups and individuals planning strikes against U.S. interests."

—9/11 COMMISSION REPORT

New Strategy

Only Had One Prong Before…Nearly Prongless

Strategy Enacted To Keep Country Safer
America blamed for sucky plan before September 11th—stupid non-cognitive geographical entity

"September the 11th changed how America must look at the world. And since that day, our nation has been on a multi-pronged strategy to keep our country safer." [37]

—GEORGE BUSH

Smoking Them Out
And Keeping The Faceless Cowards
On The Run In 1998

"First, we will use our new integrated approach to intensify the fight against all forms of terrorism: to capture terrorists, no matter where they hide; to work with other nations to eliminate terrorist sanctuaries overseas; to respond rapidly and effectively to protect Americans from terrorism at home and abroad. Second, we will launch a comprehensive plan to detect, deter, and defend against attacks on our critical infrastructures, our power systems, water supplies, police, fire, and medical services, air traffic control, financial services, telephone systems, and computer networks... Third, we will undertake a concerted effort to prevent the spread and use of biological weapons and to protect our people in the event these terrible weapons are ever unleashed by a rogue state, a terrorist group, or an international criminal organization... Finally, we must do more to protect our civilian population from biological weapons."

—BILL CLINTON, MAY 22, 1998
UNITED STATES NAVAL ACADEMY COMMENCEMENT

New Reality

Chaos Theory

Odds Not In America's Favor
Statistically, we had it coming—there's no fighting arithmetic

> *"We got to be right 100 percent of the time here at home, and they got to be right once. And that's the reality."*[38]
>
> —GEORGE BUSH

New math:
Actually, they (the terrorists) killed people in all four attacks on 9/11—al Qaeda was right four times. We (Bush) stopped them zero times...or zero percent.

Eleven...That's Quite A Few

A bin Laden plot to blow up 11 passenger jets over the Pacific Ocean was thwarted in 1995.[39]

New Awareness

2008?

McCain: We Were Only Vaguely Aware of Terrorism
Straight talk express wipes out on sharp corner in undignified fashion

> *"The awful events of September 11, 2001 declared a war we were vaguely aware of, but hadn't really comprehended how near the threat was, and how terrible were the plans of our enemies."*[40]
>
> —SENATOR JOHN MCCAIN AT THE 2004 REPUBLICAN CONVENTION

Share the bunk:
We were vaguely aware of the threat? Like who? McCain's neighbors? It's plausible that Bush didn't know what was going on—evidently that's part of his appeal, but the Senator shouldn't play dumb just to make the president appear to be less of a half-wit.

1998— Attack By Plane

The intelligence community details the infrastructure of al Qaeda in the United States. Also, intelligence information indicates bin Laden's next plan could be to fly an aircraft loaded with explosives into a U.S. airport and then detonate the plane.[41]

❖ ❖ ❖

Plastic Flowers

We Were Complacent Says McCain
Fat and sassy we was

> *"No American alive today will ever forget what happened on the morning of September 11th. That day was the moment when the pendulum of history swung toward a new era. The opening chapter was tinged with great sadness and uncertainty. It shook us from our complacency in the belief that the Cold War's end had ushered in a time of global tranquility."* [42]

—SENATOR JOHN MCCAIN AT THE 2004 REPUBLICAN CONVENTION

Xanadu:
Global tranquility? What naïve nitwit thought that? Greenie? It was Yellowie, wasn't it?

Sad song:
Very lyrical, but stupid. Swinging pendulum of history? Opening chapter? Oh please, John. Al Qaeda has been operating on a straight line for years. This is like the 150th page of very predictable book.

First Chapter Indeed

"Terrorism against our country started long before 9-11. Terrorists have been killing Americans for more than two decades." [43]

—GENERAL TOMMY FRANKS, AT THE 2004 REPUBLICAN CONVENTION

In The Very Same Speech Tommy Said...

"The attacks of Sept. 11th, brought a new enemy to our shores an enemy unlike any we've ever faced before."

New Moments

If Only There Were Some Clue

Terrorist Attack Unforeseeable
Only dozens of warnings and threats—but none on official al Qaeda letterhead

"These four years have brought moments I could not foresee and will not forget." [44]

—GEORGE BUSH AT 2004 REPUBLICAN CONVENTION

Newly Awake

Paradise Lost

Bush: Nation Was Asleep
Still tuckered out from the Macarena—let that be a dancing lesson to us all

> *"I said in my speech to a Joint Session of Congress that we are a nation awakened to danger."* [45]
>
> —GEORGE BUSH

Wake Up Call in '95

> *"Six weeks after Oklahoma City, months before—after the first antiterrorism legislation was sent by the White House to Congress, there is no further excuse for delay. Fighting terrorism is a big part of our national security today, and it will be well into the 21st century. And I ask Congress to act, and act now."*
>
> —BILL CLINTON, 1995 AIR FORCE ACADEMY SPEECH

> *"There's an old saying in Tennessee—I know it's in Texas, probably in Tennessee—that says: Fool me once, shame on— shame on you. Fool me—you can't get fooled again."*
> —GEORGE BUSH

CHAPTER FOURTEEN

American History W

"I was enthralled by history, which became my major,
with emphasis on American and European history."
—GEORGE W. BUSH "A CHARGE TO KEEP"

As part of the Bush campaign to convince the American people that everything about the 9/11 attack and al Qaeda was such a new-fangled concept that EVERYONE was in the dark, some drastic rewritings of historical fact were needed to reinforce the fairy tale of our collective ignorance.

The theme is the same throughout. Before 9/11, WE thought America was safe, but 9/11 taught us ALL a lesson, so there's really no need for anyone to take responsibility for anything.

Dream Weaver

America Lulled By Surface Peace Says Bush
Surface peace is the most dangerous peace in the peace family

> *"During the decade of the 1990s, our times often seemed peaceful on the surface. Yet beneath the surface were currents of danger. Terrorists were training and planning in distant camps... America's response to terrorism was generally piecemeal and symbolic. The terrorists concluded this was a sign of weakness, and their plans became more ambitious, and their attacks more deadly. Most Americans still felt that terrorism was something distant, and something that would not strike on a large scale in America. That is the time my opponent wants to go back to. A time when danger was real and growing, but we didn't know it...September 11, 2001 changed all that. We realized that the apparent security of the 1990s was an illusion...Will we make decisions in the light of September 11, or continue to live in the mirage of safety that was actually a time of gathering threats?"* [1]

—GEORGE BUSH

Blissfully ignorant:
The president says the danger of terrorism was there all along, but he didn't know it—and is proud to say so. He's done a heckava job.

We have a system:
The concept of government was concocted so that each citizen doesn't have to personally keep tabs on the undercurrents of danger. It doesn't matter if Allan and Edna in Dubuque thought that "terrorism was something distant."

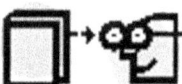

Over-Currents In 1999

"This is still a world of terror and missiles and madmen." [2]

—GEORGE BUSH,
IN A "A CHARGE TO KEEP"

It Was The Best Of Times

Little Expected Of Leaders At Times Says Bush
Still gets full pay, killer benefits and full staff of kiss-ups, though

> *"There are quiet times in the life of a nation when little is expected of its leaders. This isn't one of those times. This is a time that requires firm resolve, clear vision, and a deep faith in the values that makes us a great nation."* [3]

—GEORGE BUSH

Loophole:
Since George Bush thought the world was peaceful before 9/11 and expected little of George Bush, we should be satisfied that the little man delivered very little—because he's delighted with his performance. Makes sense.

Naïve:
No clear vision or firm resolve was needed before 9/11 according to the war president.

Do You Have Any Idea What Date It Is? I'm Trying To Get Some Sleep Here!

"It didn't start with 9/11. That was the most spectacular attack within America's borders on American soil, but this has been going on for 20 years. I mean, I don't know what to say to that. It's like saying, 'the sun rises in the west and sets in the east.' It's been attack, attack, attack." [4]

—ANN COULTER, COMMENTING ON A MICHAEL MOORE STATEMENT.

Abandon All Hope,
Yea Who Enter This Brain

An Attack Never Entered My Mind
While Growing Up Says Bush
Other than the nuclear missiles, it was perfectly safe—under my little desk

> *"And, Jordan, I wasn't sure what to think at first. You know,*
> *I grew up in a period of time where the idea of America being*
> *under attack never entered my mind—just like your Daddy's*
> *and Mother's mind probably."* [5]

—GEORGE BUSH

Unfathomable:
The number of things that never entered George Bush's mind.

Holes:
When Bush was growing up, half the country was digging fallout shelters and stocking the underground rooms with provisions to ride out any lingering radiation from the big bang.

Shared ignorance:
If Mommy and Daddy have 80+ IQ's, it's likely they weren't totally oblivious to the world around them during their youths like little George. The next time Mr. Bush insults your parents, Jordan, give him a sharp kick in the groinal area. That'll stunt his imagination.

Skeptics Of The Surface Peace Surface— Attacks Enter Minds Of Some Mommies And Daddies

A CNN/USA Today/Gallup poll in December of 1999 found that 62 percent of citizens surveyed believe terrorism is likely before the millennium New Year. [6]

Ocean Peace

The Ocean Peace Talking Points Meeting

"Okay, pipe down—here's the deal. ARI! Get that out of your nose. I've told you a hundred times—that's not funny or sanitary…good grief. Now, again—here's the plan everyone. Whenever you open your mouth, be sure to mention how the oceans have protected us and woe is us now, for they no longer keep the evildoers out. Got it? Vastness, huge oceans, what a shocker—how did they cross the vast waters and hurt us? My heavens, nobody knew the seas would let us down.

And, don't forg…WHAT!? You know, Condi, nobody gives a Karl's ass about your fancy degree. Just because you went to one of those pay attention type colleges doesn't mean you're too good to spread around some moronic manure—so just do it! Look at Don. He's not too proud—dang, he'll say anything. Colin, pay attention…you can learn something here, too."

There's Too Damn Much Lurking Going On…Stupid Lurkers

Bush: U.S. No Longer Secured By Oceans

And those uppity guard penguins have wandered off—probably should have stationed them further north

> *"The United States is no longer secure because we've got oceans. We're vulnerable to attack, as we learned so vividly. My job is to not only deal with problems, people kind of run around and lurk, my job is also to anticipate problems."*[7]

—GEORGE BUSH

It's true:

Ever since the boat was invented, we've had nothing but trouble.

What? No Ocean Peace In 1995 Either?

"The struggle against the forces of terror, organized crime and drug traf-ficking is now uppermost on our minds because of what we have endured as a nation. The World Trade Center bombing, the terrible incident in Oklahoma City, and what we have seen elsewhere—the nerve gas attack in Tokyo, the slaughter of innocent civilians by those who would destroy the peace in the Middle East, the organized crime now plaguing the former Soviet Union, so much that one of the first requests we get in every one of those countries is, send in the FBI, we need help; the drug cartels in Latin America and Asia that threaten the open societies and fragile democracies there—all these things we know can emerge from without our borders and from within our borders. Free and open societies are inherently more vulnerable to these kinds of forces. Therefore, we must remain vigilant, reduce our vulnerability, and constantly renew our efforts to defeat them."

—PRESIDENT BILL CLINTON, 1995 AIR FORCE ACADEMY SPEECH

Sharks On Atkins

Bush: We're Vulnerable To Attack

The education president teaches us all a lesson in delusional alternate theories of reality

> *"I've told you the strategic vision of our country shifted dramatically, and it shifted dramatically [after 9/11] because we now recognize that oceans no longer protect us, that we're vulnerable to attack."* [8]

—GEORGE BUSH

One If By Land, Two If By...

Bush Confident
Two Oceans Would Protect America
And a nine iron behind the front door

> *"As a matter of fact, it was very difficult to link any attack on the American soil, because prior to September the 11th, we were confident that two oceans could protect us from harm."* [9]

—GEORGE BUSH

Water on the brain:
Bush knew al Qaeda was planning an attack. He just didn't think they could pull it off with the oceans in the way. It could happen to anyone.

The Birth Of Nautical Navigation Occurred Around 3500 BC.

❖ ❖ ❖

Maybe There's Something In The Newspaper

Bush Didn't Realize
Threat Could Be Directed At Americans
Well, I'll be—he really is not a smart man

> *"It used to be that we could pick or choose whether or not we would become involved. If we saw a threat, it may be a threat to a friend, in which case we would be involved, but never did we realize the threat could be directed at the American people."* [10]

—GEORGE W. BUSH

Buffet style:
Like a smorgasbord, the president could select a small skirmish, send in the Marines to arrest a crater faced drug kingpin, or if he or she is feeling a little inadequate and needs a poll boost, bomb the crap out of an imaginary foe.

Officials Concerned About Terrorists Crossing Oceans In 90's

"In the following years (after the 1996 Olympics), the CSG designated several National Security Special Events, including the celebration of the United Nations Fiftieth Anniversary in New York, NATO's Fiftieth Anniversary in Washington, the Republican National Convention in Philadelphia, the Democratic National Convention in New York, and the 1997 and 2001 Presidential Inaugurations. Heightened security was obvious at all those events. Less obvious were the thousands of special response units with menacing-looking vehicles hidden in buildings nearby, or the hundreds of undercover federal agents on the streets, the Coast Guard cutters in the rivers, or the aircraft above." [11]

—RICHARD CLARKE
"AGAINST ALL ENEMIES"

Maybe They Used Swiftboats

Time, Distance Or Vast Oceans Won't Protect Us
And Rumsfeld is freakin' nuts—so we're pretty much screwed

> *"Time and distance from the events of September the 11th
> will not make us safer unless we act on its lessons. America is
> no longer protected by vast oceans."* [12]

—GEORGE BUSH

Curveball

9/11 Was Just A Noisy And Vivid Lesson
Imagine how the non-ocean countries feel—they're really in for it

> *"The United States is no longer secure because we've got oceans.
> We're vulnerable to attack, as we learned so vividly."* [13]

—GEORGE BUSH

Damp science:

Kansas schools are still teaching the "ocean security" theory, even though George Bush has now declared it to be a myth. "Empirical evidence my ass," said Monte Mutterman, of Hays. "I have all the faith in the world in Poseidon and the other ocean dude, the guy with the pointy pitchfork, to keep the interlopers out."

Sean, Please Explain It To George

"After all, the rising threat of global terrorism—particularly the threat of Osama bin Laden and his al Qaeda terrorist network—had been clear to U.S. policy-makers for years, from 1988 bombing of Pan Am 103 over Lockerbie, Scotland, to the 1993 World Trade Center bombing, to the 1998 bombings of two American embassies in East Africa, to the suicide attack on the USS Cole in the fall of 2000." [14]

—SEAN HANNITY, "LET FREEDOM RING"

❖ ❖ ❖

Oh, How Naïve We Was

Cheney Has Learned His Lesson
Operating only on plausible assumptions now

"Don't operate on the assumption that somehow because we live behind two oceans we're immune to attack. We now know we're not." [15]

—DICK CHENEY

Moby Dick:
"Truly, it was a hell of a shock," said Cheney. "I tried crossing the ocean once and sank like the Valdez."

Earthquake
Screws Up Ocean Protection

Rice Explains The Ocean Thing To Hughes
Word for word just like Karen wrote it

> *"I remember Condoleezza Rice saying to me, "Karen, September 11*
> *was an earthquake across the international security environment.*
> *If our oceans no longer protect us, it changes the way we have to*
> *look at everything."* [16]

—KAREN HUGHES

Tag off:
Now it's your turn Condi. "I remember Karen Hughes saying…"

She's The
Secretary Of State Now

Military Options Diminished
Now That the Oceans Have Gone Dry
And the fishing sucks

> *"You can have lots of plans but unless—since the United States sits*
> *protected by oceans, or no longer protected—the United States sits*
> *across oceans—unless you find a way to get regional cooperation from*
> *Pakistan, from the Central Asian countries, you're going to be left*
> *with essentially stand-off options, meaning bombers and cruise missiles,*
> *because you're not going to have the full range of military options."* [17]

—CONDI RICE

Spit it out:
You can say it, Condi…big oceans, sat by, sits across and so on. Even if it doesn't fit into the context of the message you're trying to convey—oh so big and watery. Unfathomable depths. Like totally wet, man.

They'll Figure How To Get Across The Atlantic Sooner Or Later

In 1999 and 2000 three blue-chip commissions issued reports. The three panels reached similar conclusions…the threat posed by terrorism is imminent.[18]

❖ ❖ ❖

Be Happy

Not Worried About Attack On Homeland
Hence the problem

> *"Well, of course, the American view of itself and its own vulnerability changed immediately. We had been protected by shores, by great oceans. We'd not had to worry about an attack on the homeland in a long, long time."* [19]

—CONDI RICE

Big ass mirror:
America viewed itself and said, "Omigosh, I'm vulnerable! My shores have gone AWOL and the oceans hardly drown anyone except for George Clooney. I should find someone who is like the fifth smartest person in his own family to lead and protect me."

Hiders

The Fargin Bastages Are Hiding!

This Enemy Hides Declares Bush
Wonders where non-hiding enemies are holed up

> *"Secondly, they [other world leaders] understand that unlike previous war, this enemy likes to hide."* [20]

> —GEORGE BUSH

Yankee Hider

General Francis Marion of South Carolina was nicknamed "The Swamp Fox" by the British because he would attack them at unexpected places and then retreat quietly into the swamps before the Redcoats could mount a counterattack. [21]

9/11 Dictated By The Past

You Can't Fight Precedent

Rummy: Tragedy Needed To Waken
Non-Secretaries of Defense lectured on security shortcomings

> *"…unfortunately history shows that it can take a tragedy like September 11th to waken to the new threats and to the need for action…"* [22]

> —DONALD RUMSFELD

Boondoggle:
Yes, it is unfortunate that it takes a tragedy for people to start doing their jobs. Almost as troubling; "Old Sleepy" and the other dozing dolts in the administration are still in charge.

Fight Terror Like It's 1999

"So I say to all of you, if we do these things—if we pursue peace, fight terrorism, increase our strength, renew our alliances—we will begin to meet our generation's historic responsibility to build a stronger 21st century America in a freer, more peaceful world."

—BILL CLINTON,
1999 STATE OF THE UNION

❖ ❖ ❖

Only Following Orders

United States Did Not Enter WWII Until 1941
Eerily—9/11 followed only 60 years later

> *"Despite Nazi Germany's repeated violations of the Versailles treaty and provocations throughout the mid 1930s, the western democracies did not take action until 1939. The U.S. government did not act against the growing threat from imperial Japan until it became all too evident at Pearl Harbor."* [23]

—CONDI RICE

Isn't it obvious?
Modeled after the Roosevelt administration, there was no way the Bush people could act on, or defend against, terrorism until Japan bombed Hawaii again.

The Germans Had Boats?

Lusitania Sunk By German Forces
Tragic event sets record for oldest 9/11 failure rationalization

> *"Despite the sinking of the Lusitania in 1915 and continued German harassment of American shipping, the United States did not enter the First World War until two years later."* [24]
>
> —CONDI RICE

That's interesting:
But it doesn't have any more to do with 9/11 than Iraq.

Victimization Of The Slow Witted

Democratic Societies
Historically Slow To Confront Threats
Electing dumber leaders might not be the solution

> *"Historically, democratic societies have been slow to react to gathering threats, tending instead to wait to confront threats until they are too dangerous to ignore or until it is too late."* [25]
>
> —CONDI RICE

Blame game:
Its society's fault that Bush wasn't prepared to deal with a terrorist attack. He's a victim of democracy.

Blame America First

Al Qaeda Emboldened
During Wimpy Reagan, Bush And Clinton Years
Masculine Bush II able to keep terrorists at bay for almost eight months

"I think you have to look back to—the '80s, and most certainly the '90s, when what was happening was that the terrorist attacks were getting bolder. They were getting more imaginative. They were getting more daring. These attacks were getting bolder and they were getting more daring. And that's because the terrorists were getting a sense of inevitability of their victory. We were not aggressively going after them. They believed that they were going to win. They saw us cut and run in Somalia. They go all the way back to the fact that the Marines left Beirut after the bombing of the—barracks. They believed that if we took casualties, we would not respond." [26]

—CONDI RICE

Really tough love:
George Bush recognizes a trend that's been developing for two decades—and what? He decides to do nothing just to make a point?

The Formerly Secret 233 Day Grace Period

Unknown to the general public, it's a historical fact that a new president needs at least 233 days in office to prepare for an attack—terrorist, nation state or space aliens. The previous 40+ chief executives were able to keep their mouths shut about this systematic flaw, for obvious reasons, but then the blabbermouths came to town...

Closed For Business

Structural Changes Needed To Defend Country
George Bush is the final piece of the puzzle

"We were in office 233 days. And the kinds of structural changes that have been needed by this country for some time did not get made in that period of time." [27]

—CONDI RICE

Lie:

No structural changes were needed within the government to defend against a hijacking or shoot down a suicide plane.

❖ ❖ ❖

ScapeGoat

Clinton Didn't Truly Declare War On al Qaeda

Bush only waited eight months—he wins

> *"How could the Bush administration be to blame in 8 months for the previous administration's failure over 8 years to truly declare war on al-Qaida?"* [28]

—SENATOR MITCH MCCONNELL

Dramatic Reenactment:

Bill Clinton says, "I truly declare war—truly I do," and Mohammed Atta and the rest of 19 al Qaeda terrorists call off the 9/11 plan to become investment bankers and little league coaches in Memphis. They raise thousands of dollars for the Cheney-Bush 2004 campaign as their way of saying thanks for the $300 tax rebate in 2001. All is well.

Old bird face:

Of course, McConnell's a moron. We could have flattened every mountain in Afghanistan to the height of Falwell's porn collection, but the 9/11 gang was living here and had the old man's credit card. When Spanky came into office, he knew the fornicator hadn't eradicated the evildoers. Bush wasn't responsible for the attacks, but he was responsible for defending against them. He agreed to handle that duty when he signed on.

At Least He Could Get Some Reading Done In There

Morris: Bad Policies At Fault For 9/11

Especially putting al Qaeda on the endangered species list—some asshole slipped that into the energy bill

> *"And you know, when you come into the White House it takes a while to find out where the bathroom is, it takes a couple months to get up to speed. And to change these policies—it's hard to turn a battleship around."* [29]

—DICK MORRIS

Oh Dick:

You whore, you.

> **"But a leader should have independently acquired understanding of the areas he oversees. Anybody who's going to take on a large organization must put time aside for deep study."**
> —RUDOLPH GIULIANI "LEADERSHIP"

CHAPTER FIFTEEN

Dots

Very Specific Information Called A Dot Is Needed To Defend the United States. The Idea Is To Connect The Dots. George Bush Requires Lots Of Dots To Do His Job.

"Tyrants and terrorists will not give us polite notice before they launch an attack on our country."[1]
—GEORGE BUSH

"Too often in government, all an employee has to do is show up and go through the motions."[2]
—RUDOLPH GIULIANI

In this scenario of self absolution, Bush argues that since he was not silver spoon fed details regarding the attacks beforehand—like the time, place and method of attack, there was nothing he could do. The terrorists had to be rooted out before they entered the airports, or the strikes were inevitable. This rationale puts all of the blame on the intelligence agencies, which was the main idea. Old loyal George would use the same people as scapegoats a few years later, too.

❖ ❖ ❖

Nostradumbass

Bush:
Four Plane Attack Never Considered By Anybody
Eleven once, but four is just plain stupid—it's not even a prime number

> *"Never (in) anybody's thought process about how to protect America did we ever think that the evildoers would fly not one, but four commercial aircraft into precious U.S. targets—never."* [3]

—GEORGE BUSH SEPT. 16, 2001

Vulcan mind meld:
Of course, that's not true, but how could a lowly chief executive get accurate information before making such a bonehead remark? A smart president might say, "Get me all the information about the use of airplanes as weapons." Then another person says, "Yes, sir!" Ten minutes later, if the unnamed person doesn't have Rove for brains and has access to a computer, the president will hold in his hands the information he requested—unless the printer jams or Cheney gets his sweaty palms on it first.

Another milestone:
Never did anyone think we would ever have a president who would be so openly pleased about his ignorance—never.

Guiding principles:
If hijackers are stopped from getting on the planes, they can't fly them into buildings. If suicide planes are shot down before they hit the targets, fewer people will be killed. If individuals are evacuated from target buildings before the suicide planes can hit, fewer people will die.

These People Thought Of It

In 1996, in security preparations for the Olympic games in Atlanta, U.S. authorities identified crop dusters and suicide flights as potential terrorist weapons. Black Hawk helicopters and U.S. Customs jets were deployed to protect Olympic venues from attack by hijacked aircraft. [4] Without a specific threat, security officials decided to defend against a possibility. Strange, but true.

Air Shows Only

Rumsfeld:
Fighter Aircraft Not Used To Protect America
Not since George W. Bush guarded the skies from the Viet Cong

> *"We have not had fighter aircraft protecting the United States*
> *for ages."* [5]

—DONALD RUMSFELD 9/16/2001

Lie:
At the very least, fighter jets
have been used since the 1996
Olympics in Atlantic to provide
protection from attacks by planes
during major events.

No Plot Needed— Just Thinking... Hmmm

Traditional defense:
Maybe we should do what is
needed to defend the country
from current threats and ditch
the "we haven't done it that way
for ages" method.

When the FBI was planning security
for the 1996 Olympic Games, they
had no specific information about
al Qaeda or a possible kamikaze
plot. "We were just thinking about
possibilities of what bad guys could
do," said an FBI Agent. [6]

Warning Schmorning

Terrorists Only Considering Hijacking
Will probably drop a card when they decide—keep your fingers crossed for
a Hallmark

> *"A warning—there was nothing that said this is going to happen, or*
> *this might happen. It said this is a method that these people might be*
> *considering. That was the nature of this. And it was very non-specific."* [7]

—CONDI RICE, REFERRING TO THE AUGUST 6TH MEMO

Empty threats:
Hell, the paper may as well have been blank! Those stupid CIA guys, with their swanky briefings and ironed shirts think they can palm off a report about bin Laden attacking the U.S. and expect us to fall for it?

Oh, warning:
The president thought you said warming. And, as you know, Bush doesn't give a rip about the temperature.

Defense Against Suicide Planes Two Months Before 9/11

Warnings were issued in July 2001 for the possibility that terrorists might try to kill George Bush and other leaders at the G-8 Summit in Genoa, by crashing an airliner into the gathering. Airspace over Genoa was closed and antiaircraft guns were positioned at the airport. No specific date, time or flight number was known.[8]

❖ ❖ ❖

They're All Talk

No Report Needed To Know Motives Of Bin Laden
But it was still a shock, though—truly surprising. Really, like totally astonishing

> *"The PDB does not say the United States is going to be attacked. It says bin Laden would like to attack the United States. I don't think you, frankly, had to have that report to know that bin Laden would like to attack the United States."*[9]

—CONDI RICE, REFERRING THE AUGUST 6TH MEMO

Smart ass:
You don't need a weather report to know it's going to rain sooner or later, either, but a little warning is nice. Some towns even prepare for flooding in advance of a thunderstorm by building dikes, drainage systems and ditches. They defend against a possible future event without knowing when it might happen. Pretty standard.

Sub-Total Recall

Intelligence Warned Of Potential Hijackings
But goodness gracious—nothing was mentioned about the color of the plane

> *"However, I don't recall receiving anything in the months prior to 9/11 that suggested terrorists might take commercial airliners and use them as missiles to fly into buildings like the World Trade Center Towers or the Pentagon."* [10]

—Donald Rumsfeld

It's futile:
Terrorists are so darn unpredictable. They've conducted suicide missions on foot, in cars, on buses, with boats and once on a water buffalo, but who could have guessed they would use a plane.

1996 Olympic Games In Atlanta—Preemptive Defense

"I called Customs and asked if they would move their p-3's (old Navy anti-submarine aircraft converted to track small planes smuggling drugs from South America) to Atlanta during the Games. I also asked if they would move in some of their Blackhawk helicopters and place Secret Service snipers with .50 caliber rifles on board to warn off, or take out, aircraft threatening the Olympics. The Defense Department agreed to set up a joint air coordination post with the FAA and to place Army radar on a hill outside of Atlanta. They also agreed to have National Guard fighter aircraft on strip alert." [11]

—RICHARD CLARKE "AGAINST ALL ENEMIES"

❖ ❖ ❖

Isn't He Adorable

"I'd Have Stopped The Attack" Says Bush

President thought they were only going to take hostages—impudent non-hostage taking evildoers

> *"Had we had the information that was necessary to stop an attack, I'd have stopped the attack. If we'd had known that the enemy was going to fly airplanes into our buildings, we'd have done everything in our power to stop it."* [12]

—GEORGE BUSH

Furthermore:
Had I known the enemy was going
to hijack airpla…D'oh!

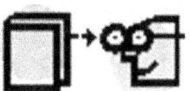

12 Reports…
That's Quite A Few

The Intelligence Community
produced at least 12 reports over a
seven-year period (94-2001)
suggesting that terrorists might
use airplanes as weapons.

—HOUSE/SENATE JOINT INQUIRY

*"One has to know that a terrorist can attack at any time
and any place using any technique."* [13]
—DONALD RUMSFELD

❖ ❖ ❖

Too Comfortable In His Own Skin

Bush Didn't Know The Enemy Would Use Airplanes
Thought they might use those little Shriner cars—beep, beep

*"Had I known that the enemy was going to use airplanes to kill on
that fateful morning, I would have done everything in my power to
protect the American people."* [14]

—GEORGE BUSH

If only there were a sign:
Maybe a written report on the subject authored by well groomed men in dark suits, or perhaps a remembrance of a time when terrorists threatened to kill me, a truly important person, with a plane—if only there had been some small hint.

❖ ❖ ❖

French Kill Hijackers

In 1994, terrorists hijacked an Air France flight with plans to blow it up over the Eiffel Tower in Paris. French troops killed the hijackers while the plane refueled in Marseilles.[15]

Kreskin

Rice: Nobody Could Have Predicted 9/11 Scenario
At least not in the same order—the heavy money was on the Pentagon to take the first hit

> *"Steve, I don't think anybody could have predicted that these people would take an airplane and slam it into the World Trade Center, take another one and slam it into the Pentagon; that they would try to use an airplane as a missile, a hijacked airplane as a missile."*[16]

—Condi Rice

Hocus Focus

"Hello Boys, I'm Baaack!"

Randy Quaid, right before using his plane as a missile to destroy an alien spaceship in the motion picture "Independence Day" 1996

Threat Warnings Principally Focused Overseas
Only partially directed at North American continent—30/70 at most

"Now, there was a clear concern that something was up, that something was coming, but it was principally focused overseas."[17]

—CONDI RICE

Condi's Choice:
Everyone knows it's impossible to defend our interests overseas AND the actual country at the same time. We probably shouldn't be spreading that around, though.

Home free:
Except for the al Qaeda cells principally located in the United States.

Clarity:
We didn't know what was coming, but were pretty sure it wasn't going to happen in the United States, so when the unknown plot was hatched, it was a shock that it didn't take place where we weren't sure it was going to unfold. A common mistake.

Parse this:
Principally focused; for the most part, but not all.

Precautions, Eh? How Does One Take These Precautions?

"There was a question of an airplane stuffed with explosives. As a result, precautions were taken."[18]

—EGYPTIAN PRESIDENT HOSNI MUBARAK, REFERRING TO THE WARNINGS OF A BIN LADEN ATTACK ON THE GENOA SUMMIT IN JULY OF 2001

Narrow Minded

Government Will Protect Citizens
If Threats Are Specific
President still rushed to Nebraska if someone sneezes in the continental U.S.

> *"Now, if we receive specific intelligence, where we—a credible threat that targets a specific building or city or facility, I can assure you our government will do everything possible to protect the citizens around and in, or near that facility."* [19]

—GEORGE BUSH

My aching Ashcroft:
What if an attacker gets sun in his eyes, or hits a bump and misses the announced target? What if they're just stupid and get the address wrong? Maybe the terrorist has a previous terror engagement that he forgot about that he can't get out of and needs to postpone the credible threat—what then? Do we downgrade the threat to a "possibly" until he makes his damn mind up, or should we remove the item from the calendar, totally wipe it off the docket, and make Mr. "my in-laws are in town, there's nothing I can do" Evildoer re-file a new threat when he can finally fit us into his precious schedule?

Hoodwinked:
Imaginary credible? Or real credible? Can it be a fantasy concoction like the threat to Air Force One, or does it have to be a threat that actually exists outside of someone's bald skull?

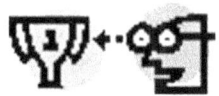

A Defense Against Suicide Planes... I'll Be Danged

Security officials for the 2000 Olympics in Sydney, Australia considered a fully fueled airliner crashing into the opening ceremonies one of their greatest fears. As a precaution, the government had six planes in the air at all times ready to intercept suspicious aircraft. Bin Laden was considered the number one threat.[20]

Intelligent Design Flaw

**Bush: Need To Know Attack Method
To Protect American People**
Typed, single spaced—no smiley faces. And, don't show it to Karl or
Scooter—I can't stress that enough

> *"The American people know this about me, and my national security
> team, and my administration: Had I known that the enemy was
> going to use airplanes to kill on that fateful morning, I would have
> done everything in my power to protect the American people."*[21]
>
> —George Bush

Conditional:
Bush isn't saying he'll defend the citizenry, but if he does, and that's big
if—he will need to know the type of conveyance prior to the assault. Tank,
sports car, Shetland pony or rickshaw—he might handle it.

The B-Team:
Indeed; the president has a whole mess of unqualified people, selected
carefully from campaign donor lists, to protect the citizens. And, of course,
the squad also includes a walk-in closet full of talented kiss-ups and
washouts from the real world. They'll be the ones you'll see on TV with
the frightened faces saying, "No one could have imagined that (someone/
something) would have done (something bad) like (method or result)."

Catch 43

Almost Never Have Specific Information Says Rice
And we can't defend without it, so that's a conspicuous problem

> *"When we talk about threats, they come in many varieties. Very often we have uncorroborated information; sometimes we have corroborated but very general information. But I can tell you that it is almost never the case that we have information that is specific as to time, place, or method of attack."* [22]

—CONDI RICE

Full circle:
The Bush administration has to know the time, place and method of attack to defend against a terrorist attack, but rarely is the threat information that specific—so what you have is a "responsibility loophole" for George and a "backwards Catch-22" for the rest of us.

"My job is to make sure that the blade is sharp." [23]
—GEORGE W. BUSH

CHAPTER SIXTEEN

Mission Impossible

Suppose Churchill had walked out from 10 Downing Street during the Battle of Britain and said, "There's really not much we can do about this."
—RUDOLPH GIULIANI "LEADERSHIP"

There was nothing they could do. It was impossible. Nineteen men carried out a plot so complicated and devious, the Bush people can think of no possible way the president could have prevented the hijackings or averted the suicide planes from reaching their targets once they were airborne. Bush is tough on terror, though—as long as nobody actually attacks.

Rubik's Cube

Hughes:
Not Even Clinton Could Have Stopped 9/11
Whoa...let's not set our standards that high

> *"I don't believe that anyone in the Bush administration—and I'm not an advocate of the Clinton administration but I'll even include them in this—I don't believe that anyone in the Clinton administration, either, could have put together the pieces before the horror of September 11. I don't think we could have envisioned it and done anything to have prevented it. If we could have in either administration, either in the eight years of the Clinton administration or the seven and a half months of the Bush administration, I'm convinced we would have done so."* [1]

—KAREN HUGHES

Paint by numbers:
What pieces? Bush knew al Qaeda had designs on hijacking American airliners and that's what they did—four times.

True believer?
Hughes is pretty sure Bush would have done something had he known of the complex plot to book a flight and hijack the plane. Let's leave it at that.

❖ ❖ ❖

Advanced Physics

Rumsfeld: Impossible To Defend Every Place
Or the Pentagon

> *"One has to know that a terrorist can attack at any time and any place using any technique. And it is not physically possible to defend in every place, at every time, against every conceivable method. We just saw the use of aircraft. It could be ships, it could be subways. It could be any number of things."* [2]
>
> —Donald Rumsfeld

Those scamps:
They caught us off guard by attacking the most obvious targets.

Big breadcrumbs:
1) Terrorists were planning to hijack planes. 2) Terrorists vowed to finish the job on the World Trade Center after a bomb failed to bring the building down in 1993. 3) Terrorists hijacked planes and crashed them into the World Trade Center.

Downer Don:
Can we at least TRY to defend against attacks with aircraft, ships and subways, even though it's impossible? Or is all the money tied up in missile shields, pomade and keeping freedom on the march?

Make It Harder To Attack Here... It's Worth A Shot

"I think that it is possible that they recognize the heightened security profile that we have post-September 11th, and I believe that we have made it harder for them to attack here."[3]

—CONDI RICE
9/11 COMMISSION TESTIMONY

Play the odds, man:
If there were only enough resources to defend three cities in the United States from a possible terrorist attack, would New York City and Washington, D.C. be on the list?

❖ ❖ ❖

Don't Expect Me To Clean Up This Mess

Rice: There Was Nothing We Could Do
Clinton's policies sucked, but we didn't want to hurt his feelings by changing them right away

> *"I would like very much to know what more could have been done given that it was an urgent problem. I don't know, Ed, how, after coming into office, inheriting policies that had been in place for at least three of the eight years of the Clinton administration, we could have done more than to continue those policies while we developed more robust policies."*[4]

—CONDI RICE ON 60 MINUTES

Police Commissioner Rice:

"Gosh Ed, the last commissioner wasn't able to eradicate crime in the ten years he was on the job, and he was smart, so I don't know what we were expected to do. We heard the convenience store would be robbed, but there wasn't any point in trying to stop it. Someone else will just rob it again next week. We decided to just let the criminals run amok until we could develop more robust policies to rub out crime once and for all."

Sleight of hand:

Clinton didn't have a policy of not defending the country. Rice intentionally confuses defense against terrorist attacks with blowing up Afghanistan, as if that would have stopped the 9/11 attacks.

Dr. Responsibility:

Perhaps Clinton should have eradicated al Qaeda, but he didn't. Your boss campaigned for the job. If he wasn't up to it, he should have stayed in Texas.

Whaaa?

If the current policies sucked and Bush thought going after al Qaeda around the globe "more robustly" would prevent an attack by the terror cells that were already in the country, what was stopping him?

Priorities:

What single thing did the Bush administration do in the first eight months that was more important than national security?

Weasel talk:

Lying to Ed Bradley is a sin.

Five years later:

How are those robust plans going?

Raising Security Levels To Thwart Hijackings And Telling The Public? ...I'm Intrigued

In December of 1999, Fox News reports of possible hijacking attempts on flights going to and from the United States. Security at all U.S. airports is at an all-time high. [5]

There's Something About Condi

Options To Defend United States Were Limited
Trying to stop a hijacking is just a waste of time and money

> *"Steps were taken, and I'm sure security steps were taken. But you have to realize that when you're dealing with something this general, there's a limit to the amount that you can do."* [6]
>
> —CONDI RICE

Don't call me Surely:
Security steps were taken—that's what she heard, anyway. Evidently, nobody would return the National Security Advisor's calls. No security steps were taken and Dr. Rice knows it.

Bullshit:
We allocate a half trillion dollars per year for defense. 500 billion. 500,000 million.

Friendly skies initiative:
Trust the airlines to handle it— that'll work. Then give them billions of dollars after they fail.

Beef Up Security At Airports? Can The President Do That Without A Specific Threat? No Time Or Place Needed? Shazaam!

Defense before dollars:
Worry about the people instead of business interests. If airline traffic slows down due to security precautions, tough luck.

> *"We have taken every precaution to make sure that it is safe to fly in America. There is beefed-up security at airports. There is increased presence on the airplanes. Yes, I would— if a family member asked whether they should fly, I'd say, yes."* [7]
>
> —GEORGE BUSH, TWO DAYS AFTER 9/11

She's A Doctor You Know

No Defense Against Hijacking Without Details
And it would have helped if the ringleaders had been featured in
People Magazine's "most interesting terrorists" issue

> *"But I think that there's always a fine balance, but even in
> retrospect, even in hindsight, there was nothing in what was briefed
> to the President that would suggest that you would go out and say to
> the American people, look, I just read that terrorists might hijack an
> aircraft. They talk about hijacking an aircraft once in a while, but
> have no specifics about when, where, under what circumstances."* [8]

—CONDI RICE

Who:
Al Qaeda.

When:
When they feel like it.

Where:
At an airport.

Under what circumstances:
They feel like it.

Hard To Find Good Help

Bush Impatiently Waits For Robust Plan
To Eradicate Al Qaeda
Asked Cheney how it was going once, though—was told to go f___ himself

> *"Bush explained to us that he had become impatient."*

—9/11 COMMISSION REPORT

Oh my! Impatience.
That's a pretty deep emotion.
Obviously the president had
some strong feelings about the
terrorism thing.

Be steadfast, dude:
Don't just sit there in the waiting
room looking at the pictures in a
Sports Illustrated. The vice president
will get back to you with the super
plan to destroy bin Laden when
he's finished with his examinations
in the secret room. You still have to
defend the country while you wait.

A Line Of Defense If Hijackers Get Through Airport Security? That's Crazy Talk!

*"And I thought I had made a
persuasive case that we needed an
air defense system as well as an
airport system, not just to stop hijackers
at baggage inspection, but to deal
with them if they got through that
and were able to hijack an aircraft."*

—RICHARD CLARKE TO
9/11 COMMISSION TALKING ABOUT
1996 ATLANTA OLYMPICS

❖ ❖ ❖

Surrender Monkey

Bush: I Needed Inkling To Defend The US
Military not enough

> *"I stepped back and I've asked myself a lot: 'Is there anything we could
> have done to stop the attacks?' Of course I've asked that question, as
> have many people in government. Nobody wants this to happen to
> America. But in the end, had I had any inkling whatsoever that the
> people were going to fly airplanes into buildings, we would have moved
> heaven and earth to save the country."* [9]

—GEORGE BUSH

Like trying to drive nails into a cue ball:

Many people got an inkling of the plan to fly airplanes into buildings after two planes flew into the Twin Towers of the World Trade Center. Too subtle?

Close enough:

Bush didn't move heaven and earth, but he moved himself through the heavens to the earth in Nebraska—then went under the earth.

Inkling

Tough self love:

Who needs God? George always forgives himself—and Karl. We'll see about Scooter and Tom in 2009.

"But as to your question about using aircraft as weapons, I was afraid beginning in 1996, not that a Cessna would fly into the Olympics, but that any size aircraft would be put into the Olympics."

Trendspotting:

Everything catches old "eagle eye" by surprise—even disasters preceded by three days of warnings on CNN.

—RICHARD CLARKE
TO 9/11 COMMISSION

❖ ❖ ❖

Failure Is An Option

Dealing With Terror Threat A Luxury Says Rice

Turning an aircraft carrier around for a photo-op is a necessity

> *"One doesn't have the luxury of dealing only with one issue if you are the United States of America. There are many urgent and important issues."* [10]

—CONDI RICE

Tunnel vision:
When the president drops everything to go on a marketing tour
for six weeks to give the same
speech over and over and over to
gain public support for one political
issue—is that a luxury?

Necessary evil:
It's al Qaeda, Condi! Can you
squeeze these guys into the busy
schedule of posing the president in
front of cameras?

Heightened Security Measures In Place— After Attacks

*"As the President indicated today
in his remarks, it is not business as
usual. And there are heightened
security and tightened security
measures in place."* [11]

—ARI FLEISCHER

Bad For Business

We Never Considered A Warning Says Rice
Had tea with the FAA, though—and some of those sticky pastry deals

> *"In the pre 9/11 period, we really never even considered issuing a
> warning. I was saying that if it had been considered, you would have
> had to consider very carefully what kind of impact you would have.
> But it was actually never considered. What was done was to get the
> FAA in the room so that they could do the things that they thought
> appropriate under these circumstances."* [12]

—CONDI RICE

Freedom of choice:
The impact Condi speaks of is the financial impact to the airline industry
if the public were let in on the hijacking threats. Money took priority over
people.

Accountability:
Evidently, nothing was appropriate. The FAA takes orders from
George W. Bush and did not raise security levels.

Not A Small World

**Needed To Know Which Cities Would Be Attacked
Says Rice**
There's no way to predict the most likely to be hit huge metropolitan areas

> *"I know that, had we thought that there was an attack coming in
> Washington or New York, we would have moved heaven and earth
> to try and stop it."*[13]

—Condi Rice

Nobody Told Us

Not Briefed On Use Of Airplanes As Weapons
Everyone knows—you can only get information in the form of a briefing

> *"To the best of my knowledge, Mr. Chairman, this kind of analysis
> about the use of airplanes as weapons actually was never briefed to us."*

—Condi Rice to 9/11 Commission

Self reliance:
A little initiative, please, Ms. National Security Advisor. Google away—
to the best of your knowledge.

Ancient History

Rice Not Aware Of Reports
Some were over two years old—dusty, allergy inducing parchments

> *"If in fact, there were some reports done in '98 and '99. I was certainly not aware of them at the time I spoke."*

—CONDI RICE TO 9/11 COMMISSION

Unreasonable doubt:
If? Oh, reports were done, Ms. Rice—lots of them—some still have that fresh toner smell.

Short term memory loss:
The boss was protected from planes crashing into the meetings at the G-8 Summit in Genoa, Italy by anti-aircraft missile batteries—only two months before 9/11.

Bush: Security Precautions Have Been Taken
Attacks already over, but nice effort…maybe before the death and destruction next time

> *"I've been in regular contact with the Vice President, the Secretary of Defense, the national security team and my Cabinet. We have taken all appropriate security precautions to protect the American people."*

—GEORGE W. BUSH
AFTERNOON OF SEPTEMBER 11, 2001

Can't Push Blood Into A Turnip

Too Much Information To Absorb Say Rice

The president is still trying to memorize the combination to his locker—and it's his date of birth

> *"...that you have thousands of pieces of information—car bombs and this method and that method—and you have to depend to a certain degree on the intelligence agencies to sort, to tell you what is actually relevant, what is based on sound sources, what is speculative."*

—CONDI RICE TO 9/11 COMMISSION

We believe the 9/11 attacks revealed four kinds of failures: in imagination, policy, capabilities, and management.
—9/11 COMMISSION REPORT

CHAPTER SEVENTEEN

The
Defense

"My job is to provide security for the American people." [1]
—GEORGE BUSH

*"We learned that the institutions charged
with protecting our borders, civil aviation, and national security
did not understand how grave this threat could be,
and did not adjust their policies, plans, and practices
to deter or defeat it."*
—9/11 COMMISSION

According to the administration, the defensive actions taken to thwart an attack consisted of the FBI trying to root out the al Qaeda cells in the U.S. and the FAA sending out some memos to the airlines. Bush also sent a stern message to Pakistan and evidently put the staff at battle stations, whatever that might entail.

Unfortunately, the 9/11 Commission could find no evidence of the FBI being tasked, the FAA didn't tighten security, President Musharaff had no luck reasoning with the Taliban and the battle hardened White House staff lost interest.

Bush's best plan, though, required wiping out al Qaeda worldwide. It sounds like a swell idea, but how he figured it to be a viable defensive measure against attacks in the meantime, there's no explanation.

Total Annihilation

I'll Bet It All, Alex

Three To Five Years Needed To Prevent 9/11 Attacks

Gosh, that might be too long—is OBL flexible with the attack date?

> *"Well, of course, you think we should have got them before they got us, but the fact of the matter is that everything that we were looking at, and, frankly, that the Clinton administration had looked at, was a 3- to 5-year plan to try to bring down al Qaida. They were hiding in Afghanistan. You had to bring down the Taliban in order to get to them. You needed stronger and better relations with Pakistan, a country with which we've had fractured relations for a number of years. And in the final analysis, the way that we are really getting them is to use military force to get them, American military force to get them, and it's not obvious that you would have been able to do that prior to 9/11."* [2]

—CONDI RICE

Crude sleight of hand:

So, the U.S. needed to eradicate al Qaeda to defend against the 9/11 hijackings? What do we do when hijackers don't have an organization to be eliminated? What if the hijacker is a disgruntled loner with poor hygiene and large pores? Is there any way to stop the smelly man?

Weak on terrorism:

If Bush felt military force was the only means to get al Qaeda and prevent a 9/11, who was stopping him? The Taliban? Was he waiting for permission from Pakistan?

This looks familiar:

The Clinton administration plan to bring down al Qaeda was written by Richard Clarke and it was given to Rice in January 2001. The Clarke plan was rejected by Bush. The new plan, which was put into action after 9/11 is said to be working out swell after only four years.

It Takes A Village Idiot

Eradication Of Al Qaeda Only Option For Bush

And bring me the heads of William Wallace, Michael Collins and Robert Roy MacGregor—hold the flies

> *"We also moved to develop a new and comprehensive strategy to try and eliminate the al-Qaida network. President Bush understood the threat, and he understood its importance. He made clear to us that he did not want to respond to al-Qaida one attack at a time. He told me he was tired of swatting flies."* [3]
>
> —CONDI RICE

Blinders:

Atta boy, George. Don't let those 50 ton Boeing houseflies distract you from the master plan. Oh sure, in the short term we're going suffer some casualties, but that's no reason to hastily safeguard against an attack before you're ready.

Trickle Down Defense

Strategy To Eliminate Al Qaeda Approved

Terrorist cells in the U.S. decide to go ahead with 9/11 plot anyway

> *"This new strategy was developed over the spring and summer of 2001 and was approved by the president's senior national security officials on September 4th. It was the very first major national security policy directive of the Bush administration—not Russia, not missile defense, not Iraq, but the elimination of al-Qaida."* [4]
>
> —CONDI RICE

FUBAR:

And? How's the September 4th plan working out? Did we stay the course or make a boneheaded turn down a dark exploding alley?

Hard to be humble:
There were no national security directives in the first eight months of the Bush era and the administration is dang proud of their lack of attention to defense for two-thirds of a year.

House Call

Rice: Plans In The Works
To Attack Enemy Where He Lives
Al Qaeda members living in the United States will be asked to move to Afghanistan where we can get a clean shot at them

> *"Our [pre-9/11 National Security Presidential Directive] plan called for military options to attack al Qaeda and Taliban leadership, ground forces and other targets—Taking the fight to the enemy where he lived."*

—NATIONAL SECURITY ADVISER CONDOLEEZZA RICE, TO 9/11 COMMISSION

Short attention span:
And maybe we'll bomb the bejeezus out of a country where al Qaeda doesn't live just for laughs, to see if y'all are paying attention.

Omigosh...

9/11 Commissioner
Jamie Gorelick:
"Is it true, as Dr. Rice said, 'Our plan called for military options to attack Al Qaida and Taliban leadership'?"

Deputy Secretary of State
Richard Armitage:
"No, I think that was amended after the horror of 9/11."

—9/11 COMMISSION REPORT

Information Circulars

Circular Logic

Flyer Sent To Airlines Warning Of Hijackings
Defense of country delegated to profit motivated corporations that file for bankruptcy about twice a year

> *"Now, the FAA was also concerned of threats to U.S. citizens such as airline hijackings, and therefore, issued an information circular—an information circular goes out to the private carriers from law enforcement—saying that we have a concern. That was a June 22nd information circular."* [5]

—CONDI RICE

Guerilla marketing:
"Hey Orangey! Send out some handbills to the airlines and put a few under the wiper blades of the planes in the parking lot, will ya?"

Way harsh:
"We have a concern." It's astonishing the airlines didn't take such a strongly worded message more seriously.

Bold Leadership

Another Memo Sent To Airlines
Companies strongly "urged" to use caution—if they're so inclined

> *"On July 18th, the FAA issued another IC, saying that there were ongoing terrorist threats overseas, and that although there were no specific threats directed at civil aviation, they told the airlines, 'we urge you to use the highest level of caution.'"* [6]

—CONDI RICE

Wink wink:
Is that a quote? Did the memo say there were no specific threats? Perfect—except for the specific terrorists training to specifically hijack planes.

Red Flag

Terror Groups Planning And Training For Hijackings
But don't worry about it too much—nothing mandatory, just thought we
would mention it—in case it somehow applied to the airline business

> *"At the end of July, the FAA issued another IC, which said, there's
> no specific target, no credible info of attack to U.S. civil aviation
> interests, but terror groups are known to be planning and training
> for hijackings, and we ask you, therefore, to urge—to use caution."*[7]

—CONDI RICE

Big leap:
Terrorists are planning and training
for hijackings—I wonder what
they could be up to? Perhaps we
should urge something?

The FAA Doesn't Increase Security

—9/11 COMMISSION

Battle Stations

Summer School
At Battle Stations In June And July Says Rice
But, of course the president went on vacation all of August—and then
back to school, so you know

> *"In June and July when the threat spikes were so high…
> we were at battle stations."*

—NATIONAL SECURITY ADVISER CONDOLEEZZA RICE TO 9/11 COMMISSION

Wishy washy terrorists:
When nothing happened by August we figured they had lost interest.

Great Expectations

President Expected Rumsfeld To Provide
Force Protection
And to lasso varmints

> *"And the president of the United States had us at battle station during this period of time. He expected his secretary of state to be locking down embassies. He expected his secretary of defense to be providing force protection."* [8]
>
> —Condi Rice

Almost a quorum:
Rumsfeld said it wasn't his problem, so the Secretary probably wasn't fully on-board with the force protection thing, but the embassies were locked tight—airtight, even dead-bolted.

Man the Copiers

Hadley: Threats To Homeland Not Ruled Out
We made little forts with the office supplies—it was pretty neat

> *"And at that point various alerts went out from the Federal Aviation Administration to the FBI saying the intelligence suggests a threat overseas. We don't want to be caught unprepared. We don't want to rule out the possibility of a threat to the homeland. And therefore preparatory steps need to be made. So the president put us on battle stations."* [9]
>
> —Stephen Hadley Deputy National Security Advisor

War games:
At battle stations, and yet the president was still caught unprepared. Good grief, there were thousands of those sticky memo things on the walls and computers with "We don't want to be caught unprepared. We don't want to rule out the possibility of a threat to the homeland" written on them.

Code zero:

When are there no potential threats to the country? Are there times when there is no possibility of an attack or disaster, and everyone takes five weeks off at the same time? Is it always August?

❖ ❖ ❖

High On Life

Rice:
Everyone On A Heightened State Of Alert On 9/11

One notch higher than usual "coma" level

> *"Throughout July and August, several times a week, there were meetings of the CSG, reviewing information at hand. There was no specific new information that came in in that period of time after the end of July and sort of in August, leading up to September. But the agencies were still at a heightened state of alert. Particularly overseas. I think the military actually had dropped its state of alert, but everybody was still on a heightened state of alert."* [10]

—CONDI RICE

Sedated:

Bush, Rumsfeld and Rice went back to their regular schedules after the first attack. They were on such a high state of alert, a commercial airliner slamming into the World Trade Center didn't even trigger a bad vibe.

FBI

Baby Steps

Rice: FBI Tasked To Quash Al Qaeda Threat

Well, that takes care of the terrorist problem—tax cuts for the house!

"The country had already taken steps through the FBI to task their 56 field offices to increase their activity. The country had taken the steps that it could given that there was no threat reporting about what might happen inside the United States." [11]

—CONDI RICE

Talking geographical entity?
The country took steps? Don't try to palm this off on a land mass with defined borders and a flag, Condi.

Built-in scapegoat:
What if the FBI can't break up the terrorist cells before an attack?

Depends on the meaning of threat:
The title of the August 6, 2001 President's Daily Brief was "Bin Laden Determined to Attack Inside the United States"

Oh Condi... Not Again?

"We have done thousands of interviews here at the 9/11 Commission. We've gone through literally millions of pieces of paper. To date, we have found nobody— nobody at the FBI who knows anything about a tasking of field office." [12]

—9/11 COMMISSIONER ROEMER

Strong Words

Testy Telegram

Strong Message Sent To Pakistan
Had one of those frowny face stickers on the envelope

"Within a month of taking office, President Bush sent a strong private message to President Musharraf, urging him to use his influence with the Taliban to bring bin Laden to justice and to close down al-Qaida training camps." [13]

—CONDI RICE

Pansy:
And? How did that go—asking for permission to defend the country?

Feel the burn:
Why not close down the training camps with some big explosions? It's not like we have a shortage of bombs.

Everything That Could Be Done Was Done

Loose Shoes

President Did Everything He Could Says Rice
Considering his limited abilities, how much did you really expect?

> *"But this President, who takes extremely seriously the security of the United States, was doing everything that he could in this period, as were the rest of the public servants in this government."* [14]

—CONDI RICE

To infinity and beyond:
The president did everything? Is that an itemized list?

Rubber not hitting road:
George takes security seriously, but that's probably not enough. Oh, he cares so much it hurts.

Texas leaguer:
Bush probably did do everything he was capable of—that's the problem.

The Grownups Are In Charge

Rice: "I'm Sure Security Steps Were Taken"
But don't hold me to that—it's not really my job to know these things

"Steps were taken, and I'm sure security steps were taken." [15]

—CONDI RICE

The Bush Defense Recap:

The defense mounted by the Bush administration was mainly theoretical and/or imaginary. No additional security precautions were taken to prevent a hijacking. When the hijackings were discovered, it was obvious that no one at the FAA had been primed to be on the lookout for the takeover of a plane. When the military was finally informed of the events taking place in the sky, they certainly weren't prepared to act quickly. In spite of the warnings of potential hijackings by an ultra violent terrorist organization, George Bush didn't prepare himself, let alone the government agencies under his control.

"Leaders may possess brilliance, extraordinary vision,
fate, even luck. Those help; but no one, no matter how gifted,
can perform without careful preparation, thoughtful experiment,
and determined follow-through."
—RUDOLPH GIULIANI "LEADERSHIP"

CHAPTER EIGHTEEN

Problem
Solved

"He (President George W. Bush) said that if his advisors had told him there was a (terrorist) cell in the United States, they would have moved to take care of it."
—GEORGE BUSH TO 9/11 COMMISSION

Well, there you have it. If George W. Bush had known there were al Qaeda cells in the country, he would have taken care of it. Problem solved. No cells, no hijackings, no 9/11.

Cheney knew. Rice knew. Steven Hadley and Colin Powell were briefed about the cells. The president's August 6th daily brief said there were terrorist cells in the country. News organizations, including Bush's favorite network reported on the subject. But, somehow—somehow the information didn't make it through the filter to the president. Maybe one of his people could compile the things he should know on a DVD and sprinkle in a few cartoons to keep Homer's attention.

The Incredible Denseness Of Being

President Aware Of Issues
Stand back everyone—he may be about to say something folksy

> *"I remember very well that the president was aware that there were issues inside the United States. He talked to people about this. But I don't remember the Al Qaida cells as being something that we were told we needed to do something about."*
>
> —Condi Rice to 9/11 Commission

Sworn to secrecy:
"I'm sorry Mr. President, but we can't tell you what the issues are. Frankly, we've probably told you more than you can comprehend, already."

August 6, 2001 Presidential Daily Brief

Al Qaeda members—including some who are U.S. citizens—have resided in or traveled to the U.S. for years, and the group apparently maintains a support structure that could aid attacks.

Some Call Me The Space Cowboy

President Heartened By Investigations
Although FBI won't tell him what they are investigating—you know...Karl

> *"He (Bush) recalled some operational data on the FBI, and remembered thinking it was heartening that 70 investigations were under way."*
>
> —9/11 Commission Report

Curious George:
He was heartened? Well that's just swell. A sentient being might find a high number of investigations on one issue alarming and ask what the issue is.

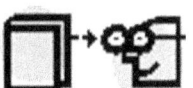

August 6, 2001 Presidential Daily Brief

CIA and the FBI are investigating a call to our embassy in UAE in May saying that a group of bin Laden supporters was in the U.S. planning attacks with explosives.

Outsider

White House Staff Briefed On Sleeper Cells
Commander-in-Chief catching some rays on the presidential veranda

> *"During the transition, Clarke briefed Secretary of State-designate Powell, Rice, and Hadley on al Qaeda, including a mention of "sleeper cells" in many countries, including the United States. Clarke gave a similar briefing to Vice President Cheney in the early days of the administration."*

—9/11 COMMISSION REPORT

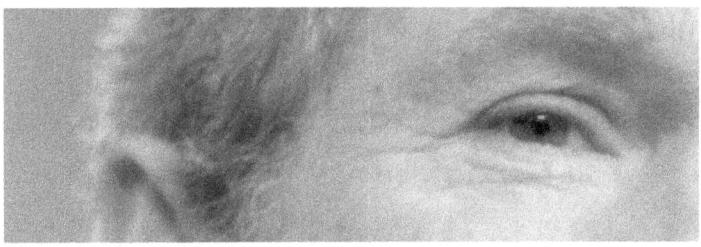

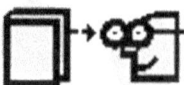

August 6, 2001
Presidential Daily Brief

Nevertheless, FBI information since (1998) that time indicates patterns of suspicious activity in this country consistent with preparations for hijackings or other types of attacks, including recent surveillance of federal buildings in New York.

❖ ❖ ❖

The Information Was Trapped
In The Bowels Of The Document

FBI Pursues Sleeper Cells In United States
Only 70 investigations, though—nothing too serious

> *"And I also understood that that was what the FBI was doing, that the FBI was pursuing these al-Qaida cells. I believe in the August 6th memorandum it says that there were 70 full field investigations under way of these cells."* [1]

—CONDI RICE

❖ ❖ ❖

Case Mother Lode

Rice: 56 FBI Field Offices On Terrorism Cases
Sell when it hits 60

> *"Rice told us she understood that the FBI had tasked its 56 US field offices to increase surveillance of suspected terrorists and to reach out to informants who might have information about terrorist plots."*

—9/11 COMMISSION REPORT

Oh, Thooose Sleeper Cells

Rice Knew About Al Qaeda Cells In U.S.
They're not over there, so we might need to fight them over here

> *"In the memorandum that Dick Clarke sent me on January 25th,
> he mentions sleeper cells."*

—CONDI RICE TO 9/11 COMMISSION

Like A Smartass Kid:
"You just told me the garbage can was full; you didn't say I needed to take it out."

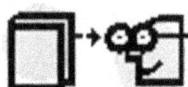

August 6, 2001 Presidential Daily Brief

The FBI is conducting approximately 70 full field investigations throughout the U.S. that it considers bin Laden-related.

O'Reilly Knew

Fox News: Bin Laden's People In The U.S.
Probably here on holiday—a happy holiday

> *"Intelligence officials tell FOX NEWS they have information that
> in the past two months hundreds of bin Laden's operatives have left his
> training camps in Afghanistan and elsewhere to various locations
> around the globe, including the U.S."*[2]

—RITA COSBY FOX NEWS DECEMBER 28, 1999

Saving Private Bush

Rice Doesn't Recall Conversation With President
It's just steadfast this, steadfast that—blah, blah, blah, all day long

> *Question:*
> Did you tell the president, at any time prior to August 6th, of the
> existence of al-Qaida cells in the United States?
>
> *"I really don't remember, Commissioner, whether I discussed this
> with the president."*
>
> —Condi Rice to 9/11

Quo:
I smell a promotion and some lapel hardware.

---

*"From January 20th through September 10th, the president received at
these daily meetings more than 40 briefing items on al-Qaida, and 13
of those were in response to questions he or his top advisers posed."*[3]

—Condi Rice

*"I'm the commander—see, I don't need to explain—
I do not need to explain why I say things.
Maybe somebody needs to explain to me why they say something,
but I don't feel like I owe anybody an explanation."*[4]
—George Bush

Epilogue

In his book "The Right Man—an Inside Account of the Bush White House" former Bush speechwriter David Frum offers his take on the president's 9/11 performance.

> *"There would be much criticism of Bush's seeming disorientation and unease in the early hours after the attack. Well, who that day wasn't disorientated and uneasy?"*

That's a pretty good excuse. Poor George, just an average guy minding his own business—he's not superhuman for crying out loud. Nobody could be expected to stay focused and do their duty under such severe circumstances. All great leaders get confused and anxious when under pressure, and then hide. Everybody does it.

Well, not everyone—when actually compared to other regular folk, it turns out that the hypothetically heroic Bush ranked mucho notches below mediocre on the bewilderment scale. Plenty of people right in the midst of fire, smoke, crumbling buildings and lunatics with knives, weren't disorientated on 9/11 and were able to function—unlike the Commander-in-Chief— AKA "The Right Man." And, other than the president—evidently no one else in the nation felt compelled to make a bee line for Nebraska for safety reasons.

Thousands of emergency professionals and ordinary citizens kept their heads and immediately went to the aid of others. The first responders in New York and Washington, D.C. were not disorientated as they ran towards danger to do their job—saving lives. According to the 9/11 Commission, flight attendants stayed calm, relating information to the ground in the midst of violent hijackings. The passengers on Flight 93 figured out the plan of the attackers in short order—then took direct action.

Americans impulsively help others in need—at risk to their own life if necessary. On 9/11, Bush's instincts told him to continue with his regular schedule—and then get to 50,000 feet ASAP.

Even those wise to George Bush's limited talents, laziness and egocentric personality were surprised by the totality of his breakdown—Bush was able to descend even below the lowest of low expectations and set a new standard for ineptitude.

What came next, though, was classic Bush and unsurprising to anyone familiar with the Bullshit Artist. George would lie, deny, stall, scapegoat and threaten—knowing that by the time the truth dripped out on page 16, he would be miles down the road and rationalizing his latest fiasco.

Leaders naturally lead during a crisis—not behave like a lost child at the mall. George Bush certainly doesn't represent the best of America. He couldn't handle the daily schedule of most people—let alone perform competently as the President and Commander-in-Chief during a disaster.

Millions of people in this country work two or three jobs to make ends meet. They don't have servants to wash their clothes, shop for groceries, cook, mow the lawn, shovel the snow, clean the gutters, guard the kids, paint the house, drive them to work, fly them anywhere, wash their dishes, pick up the dry cleaning or go to the bank. Many don't get vacation time—ever!

With all of his time freed up to be president—a job he asked for, George W. Bush couldn't learn—or wouldn't learn the basics of his job. Regular citizens, those who know what it's like to work for a living, manage to learn their jobs and do them well—even with all of the other daily responsibilities on their shoulders. If they don't perform well at work, they get fired. Accountability, responsibility, character, integrity and sense of duty are not merely talking points in the real world.

What would you do if chosen to be the President of the United States for the next four years? Aside from the honor, you would get $400,000 a year, plus perks, a lifetime pension and be allowed to throw water balloons at your jackass neighbor from Marine One.

Would you start planning your first vacation or hit the books and learn the responsibilities of the job? Would you do the 9-5 thing with the three day weekends—or be alert and prepared at all times? If terrorists attacked, would you immediately fight the threat and defend the people—or ponder the problem while finishing a photo op?

Knowing what the Bushman considers a job well done—my money is on you. Of course, a chimp with a hangover could have bettered George Bush's performance on 9/11.

We don't need to get carried away and expect Border Collie type smarts, but is it too inconvenient for the political parties to put forward a semi-intelligent presidential candidate who doesn't misremember, misspeak or blatantly lie every time he speaks? Can they at least try to recruit a person willing to spend a full four years on the job—and who isn't only shooting for the perks and a grand entrance at the next class reunion?

Can the powers that decide to facilitate the installation of a malleable empty Armani into the high office to do their bidding at least try to find a carcass that isn't a total stiff?

Can more of the voters at least try to find out some details about the candidates and use some common sense? Perhaps judge the candidate as you would someone you just met on the street and trust your instincts. If the person stumbles over words, rambles nonsensically and appears to be an idiot—they are quite probably an idiot and their lack of brain power could possibly cause problems down the road.

If you see dozens of people/pundits on television trying to convince you that a certain person isn't stupid—the person is dumber than you can possibly imagine.

And if you wouldn't trust the person to manage your business, watch your tropical fish for the afternoon or clip the neighbors hedges—the person is probably untrustworthy and unqualified to be the leader of the free world.

This country needs more statesmen—and fewer liars, weasels and bullshit artists. It's a matter of life and death.

AND THE BEAT GOES ON...

DECEMBER 2, 2005
"Before 9-11, both the Clinton and Bush administrations
said they had identified Osama bin Laden and al-Qaida
as problems that have to be dealt with, and were working on it,
but they just were not very high on their priority list.
And again it seems that the safety of the American people
is not very high on Washington's priority list."
—9/11 COMMISSION CHAIRMAN THOMAS KEAN

Notes

Chapter 1

[1]Tom Bayles, Sarasota Herald-Tribune September 10, 2002

[2]The 9/11 Commission Report: Final Report of the National Commission on Terrorist Attacks Upon the United States (New York: W.W. Norton & Company), p5.

[3]The 9/11 Commission Report: Final Report of the National Commission on Terrorist Attacks Upon the United States (New York: W.W. Norton & Company), p19.

[4]The 9/11 Commission Report: Final Report of the National Commission on Terrorist Attacks Upon the United States (New York: W.W. Norton & Company), p20.

[5]Jim Dwyer, Kevin Flynn, 102 Minutes: The Untold Story of the Fight to Survive Inside the Twin Towers (New York: Times Books, 2005), p19.

[6]The 9/11 Commission Report: Final Report of the National Commission on Terrorist Attacks Upon the United States (New York: W.W. Norton & Company), p21.

[7]Jim Dwyer, Kevin Flynn, 102 Minutes: The Untold Story of the Fight to Survive Inside the Twin Towers (New York: Times Books, 2005), p19.

[8]Secretary Rumsfeld Interview for ABC News This Week Sunday, September 16, 2001

[9]The 9/11 Commission Report: Final Report of the National Commission on Terrorist Attacks Upon the United States (New York: W.W. Norton & Company), p21.

[10]Ibid., p9.

[11]Bill Sammon, Washington Times October 7, 2002

Chapter 2

[1]Bill Sammon, Washington Times October 7, 2002

[2]Ari Fleischer Press Gaggle, Knoxville News Sentinel, September 11, 2001

[3]Rudolph W. Giuliani, Leadership (New York: Miramax Books, 2002), p143.

[4]John Diamond and Kathy Kiely, USA TODAY, May 17, 2002, www.usatoday.com/news/washington/2002/05/17/failure-usatcov.htm

[5]Bill Sammon, Washington Times October 7, 2002

[6]Bob Woodward, Bush At War (New York: Simon & Schuster, 2002), p4.

[7]Richard A. Clarke, Against All Enemies: Inside America's War On Terror (New York: Free Press, 2004), p1.

[8]Bill Sammon, The Washington Times October 7, 2002

[9]The 9/11 Commission Report: Final Report of the National Commission on Terrorist Attacks Upon the United States (New York: W.W. Norton & Company), p35.

[10]Bob Woodward, Bush At War (New York: Simon & Schuster, 2002), p136.

[11]David Gregory interviews Karen Hughes, September 11, 2002, MSNBC www.msnbc.com/modules/91102/interviews/hughes.asp?0cb=-21a105678&cp1=1

[12]Christopher Andersen, George And Laura: Portrait of an America Marriage (New York: William Morrow, 2002), p4.

[13]The 9/11 Commission Report: Final Report of the National Commission on Terrorist Attacks Upon the United States (New York: W.W. Norton & Company), p35.

[14]David Gregory interviews Condi Rice, September 11, 2002, MSNBC www.msnbc.com/modules/91102/interviews/rice.asp?0cb=-41a105678&cp1=1

[15]John Diamond and Kathy Kiely, USA TODAY, May 17, 2002, www.usatoday.com/news/washington/2002/05/17/failure-usatcov.htm

[16]Campbell Brown interviews Karl Rove, September 11, 2002, MSNBC www.msnbc.com/modules/91102/interviews/rove.asp?0cb=-51a105678&cp1=1

[17]The 9/11 Commission Report: Final Report of the National Commission on Terrorist Attacks Upon the United States (New York: W.W. Norton & Company), p260.

[18]Campbell Brown interviews Karl Rove, September 11, 2002, MSNBC www.msnbc.com/modules/91102/interviews/rove.asp?0cb=-51a105678&cp1=1

[19]The News with Brian Williams, CNBC September 9, 2002

[20]Rudolph W. Giuliani, Leadership (New York: Miramax Books, 2002, p4.

[21]Ari Fleischer, Press Gaggle Transcript, Knoxville News Sentinel, September 11, 2001

[22]Ari Fleischer, Taking Heat: The President, the Press, and My Years in the White House (New York: William Morrow, 2005), p139.

[23]www.americanprogress.org/site/pp.asp?c=biJRJ8OVF&b=40520

[24]Ari Fleischer Press Gaggle Transcript, Knoxville News Sentinel, September 11, 2001

[25]Karen Hughes, Ten Minutes From Normal (New York: Penguin Group, 2004), p234.

[26]Associated Press, August 19, 2002

[27]http://www.msnbc.msn.com/id/4693224/

[28]Jim Dwyer, Kevin Flynn, 102 Minutes: The Untold Story of the Fight to Survive Inside the Twin Towers (New York: Times Books, 2005), p78.

[29]The 9/11 Commission Report: Final Report of the National Commission on Terrorist Attacks Upon the United States (New York: W.W. Norton & Company), p22.

Chapter 3

[1]Rudolph W. Giuliani, Leadership (New York: Miramax Books, 2002, p144.

[2]Meet the Press 9/16/2001

[3]David Gregory interviews Karen Hughes, September 11, 2002, MSNBC www.msnbc.com/modules/91102/interviews/hughes.asp?0cb=-21a105678&cp1=1

[4]David Gregory interviews Condi Rice, September 11, 2002, MSNBC /www.msnbc.com/modules/91102/interviews/rice.asp?0cb=-41a105678&cp1=1

[5]The News with Brian Williams, CNBC September 9, 2002

[6]60 Minutes, www.cbsnews.com/stories/2004/03/19/60minutes/main607356.shtml

[7]The News with Brian Williams, CNBC September 9, 2002

[8]60 Minutes II www.cbsnews.com/stories/2002/09/11/60II/main521718.shtml

[9]Bill Sammon, Fighting Back: The War On Terrorism-From Inside the Bush White House (Washington, DC: Regnery Publishing, 2002), p88.

[10]Fahrenhype 9/11Companion Book, Edited by Lee Troxler, p135.

[11]Bill Sammon, Washington Times October 7, 2002

[12]Bob Woodward, Bush At War (New York: Simon & Schuster, 2002), p15.

[13]60 Minutes II, www.cbsnews.com/stories/2002/09/11/60II/main521718.shtml

[14]Ari Fleischer, Taking Heat: The President, the Press, and My Years in the White House (New York: William Morrow, 2005), p.140.

[15]Bill Sammon, Washington Times October 7, 2002

[16]Ibid

[17]Sean Hannity, Let Freedom Ring: Winning The War of Liberty Over Liberalism (New York: ReganBooks, 2002) p12.

[18]Christopher Andersen, George And Laura: Portrait of an America Marriage (New York: William Morrow, 2002), p3.

[19]Bob Woodward, Bush At War (New York: Simon & Schuster, 2002), p15.

[20]Bill Sammon, Fighting Back: The War On Terrorism-From Inside the Bush White House (Washington, DC: Regnery Publishing, 2002), p88.

Chapter 4

[1]60 Minutes II,
www.cbsnews.com/stories/2002/09/11/60II/main521718.shtml

[2]Bob Woodward, Bush At War (New York: Simon & Schuster, 2002), p342.

[3]The News with Brian Williams, CNBC September 9, 2002

[4]Bill Sammon, Washington Times October 7, 2002

[5]John Leach, 2004 article published in Aviation, Space, and Environmental Medicine, Time Magazine, May 2, 2005

[6]Bob Woodward, Bush At War (New York: Simon & Schuster, 2002), p38.

[7]Bill Sammon, Fighting Back: The War On Terrorism-From Inside the Bush White House (Washington, DC: Regnery Publishing, 2002), p90.

[8]Ibid., p90.

[9]Bob Woodward, Bush At War (New York: Simon & Schuster, 2002), p158.

[10]Scot J. Paltrow, Wall Street Journal

[11]George W. Bush, A Charge To Keep (New York: William Morrow & Company, Inc., 1999)

[12]Christopher Andersen, George And Laura: Portrait of an America Marriage (New York: William Morrow, 2002), p3.

[13]Bob Woodward, Bush At War (New York: Simon & Schuster, 2002), p259.

[14]Ari Fleischer, Taking Heat: The President, the Press, and My Years in the White House (New York: William Morrow, 2005), p140.

[15]Bill Sammon, Fighting Back: The War On Terrorism-From Inside the Bush White House (Washington, DC: Regnery Publishing, 2002), p84.

[16]Campbell Brown interviews Karl Rove, September 11, 2002, MSNBC www.msnbc.com/modules/91102/interviews/rove.asp?0cb=-51a105678&cp1=1

[17]Ari Fleischer, Taking Heat: The President, the Press, and My Years in the White House (New York: William Morrow, 2005), p 140.

[18]Patrick D. Healy, New York Times, June 23, 2005

[19]Bill Sammon, Fighting Back: The War On Terrorism-From Inside the Bush White House (Washington, DC: Regnery Publishing, 2002), p85.

[20]Bill Sammon, Fighting Back: The War On Terrorism-From Inside the Bush White House (Washington, DC: Regnery Publishing, 2002), p85.

[21]Ibid. p85.

[22]www.jewishworldreview.com/cols/coulter110101.asp

[23]Bill Sammon, Fighting Back: The War On Terrorism-From Inside the Bush White House (Washington, DC: Regnery Publishing, 2002), p85.

[24]The News With Brian Williams CNBC, September 9, 2002

[25]Carolyn B. Thompson, James W. Ware, The Leadership Genius Of George W. Bush: 10 Commonsense Lessons from the Commander in Chief (New Jersey: John Wiley & Sons, Inc., 2003), p117.

[26]60 Minutes II, September 11, 2002

[27]Bill Sammon, Fighting Back: The War On Terrorism-From Inside the Bush White House (Washington, DC: Regnery Publishing, 2002)

[28]Fahrenhype 9/11Companion Book, Edited by Lee Troxler, p47.

[29]Fahrenhype 9/11Companion Book, Edited by Lee Troxler, p111.

[30]Fahrenhype 9/11Companion Book, Edited by Lee Troxler, p134.

[31]Fahrenhype 9/11Companion Book, Edited by Lee Troxler, p134.

[32]Fahrenhype 9/11Companion Book, Edited by Lee Troxler, p134.

Chapter 5

[1]Campbell Brown interviews Karl Rove, September 11, 2002 MSNBC www.msnbc.com/modules/91102/interviews/rove.asp?0cb=-51a105678&cp1=1

[2]George W. Bush, A Charge To Keep (New York: William Morrow & Company, Inc., 1999)

[3]Campbell Brown interviews Karl Rove, September 11, 2002, MSNBC www.msnbc.com/modules/91102/interviews/rove.asp?0cb=-51a105678&cp1=1

[4]60Minutes II www.cbsnews.com/stories/2002/09/11/60II/main521718.shtml

[5]http://archives.cnn.com/2001/US/09/11/chronology.attack/

[6]Bill Sammon, Fighting Back: The War On Terrorism-From Inside the Bush White House (Washington, DC: Regnery Publishing, 2002), p 93.

[7]CNN.com, http://archives.cnn.com/2001/US/09/11/chronology.attack/

[8]Campbell Brown interviews Karl Rove, September 11, 2002, MSNBC www.msnbc.com/modules/91102/interviews/rove.asp?0cb=-51a105678&cp1=1

[9]Bill Sammon, Fighting Back: The War On Terrorism-From Inside the Bush White House (Washington, DC: Regnery Publishing, 2002), p93.

[10]Ibid., p93.

[11]Carolyn B. Thompson, James W. Ware, The Leadership Genius Of George W. Bush: 10 Commonsense Lessons from the Commander in Chief (New Jersey: John Wiley & Sons, Inc., 2003), p 174.

[12]Ibid., p93.

[13]Ari Fleischer, Taking Heat: The President, the Press, and My Years in the White House (New York: William Morrow, 2005), p140.

[14]Meet the Press 9/16/2001

[15]www.whitehouse.gov

[16]60 Minutes II, September 11, 2002, www.cbsnews.com/stories/2002/09/11/60II/main521718.shtml

[17]Bill Sammon, Fighting Back: The War On Terrorism-From Inside the Bush White House (Washington, DC: Regnery Publishing, 2002), p94.

[18]Ibid., p95.

[19]Bob Woodward, Bush At War (New York: Simon & Schuster, 2002), p16.

[20]Bill Sammon, Fighting Back: The War On Terrorism-From Inside the Bush White House (Washington, DC: Regnery Publishing, 2002), p94.

[21]Karen Hughes, Ten Minutes From Normal (New York: Penguin Group, 2004), p235.

[22]Ari Fleischer, Taking Heat: The President, the Press, and My Years in the White House (New York: William Morrow, 2005), p140.

Chapter 6

[1]The 9/11 Commission Report: Final Report of the National Commission on Terrorist Attacks Upon the United States (New York: W.W. Norton & Company), p39.

[2]Bill Sammon, Fighting Back: The War On Terrorism-From Inside the Bush White House (Washington, DC: Regnery Publishing, 2002), p98.

[3]Ibid., p107.

[4]Campbell Brown interviews Karl Rove, September 11, 2002, www.msnbc.com/modules/91102/interviews/rove.asp?0cb=-51a105678&cp1=1

[5]Campbell Brown interviews Karl Rove, September 11, 2002, www.msnbc.com/modules/91102/interviews/rove.asp?0cb=-51a105678&cp1=1

[6]David Gregory interviews Condi Rice, September 11, 2002, www.msnbc.com/modules/91102/interviews/rice.asp?0cb=-41a105678&cp1=1

[7]Secretary Rumsfeld Interview for ABC News This Week, September 16, 2001, www.defenselink.mil/transcripts/2001/t09162001_t0916sd.html

[8]News Telegraph, www.telegraph.co.uk/news/main.jhtml?xml=%2Fnews%2F2001%2F12%2F16%2Fwbush16.xml

[9]Donald Rumsfeld, DoD News Briefing, September 27, 2001, www.defenselink.mil/transcripts/2001/t09272001_t0927sda.html

[10]Bill Sammon, Fighting Back: The War On Terrorism-From Inside the Bush White House (Washington, DC: Regnery Publishing, 2002), p101.

[11]Donald Rumsfeld, DoD News Briefing, September 27, 2001, www.defenselink.mil/transcripts/2001/t09272001_t0927sda.html

[12]Scot Paltrow, Wall Street Journal March 22, 2004

[13]Christopher Andersen, George And Laura: Portrait of an America Marriage (New York: William Morrow, 2002), p5.

[14]Bill Sammon, Fighting Back: The War On Terrorism-From Inside the Bush White House (Washington, DC: Regnery Publishing, 2002), p101.

[15]Christopher Andersen, George And Laura: Portrait of an America Marriage (New York: William Morrow, 2002), p8.

[16]Bob Woodward, Bush At War (New York: Simon & Schuster, 2002), p19.

Chapter 7

[1] Bill Sammon, Fighting Back: The War On Terrorism-From Inside the Bush White House (Washington, DC: Regnery Publishing, 2002), p119.

[2] Ibid., p130.

[3] Seinfeld Episode no. 84 "The Fire" (Original air date 5 May 1994) www.seinfeldscripts.com/TheFire.html

[4] Secretary Rumsfeld Interview for ABC News This Week, September 16, 2001, www.defenselink.mil/transcripts/2001/t09162001_t0916sd.html

[5] The News With Brian Williams CNBC, September 9, 2002

[6] Ibid

[7] Carolyn B. Thompson, James W. Ware, The Leadership Genius Of George W. Bush: 10 Commonsense Lessons from the Commander in Chief (New Jersey: John Wiley & Sons, Inc., 2003), p37.

[8] 60 Minutes II, September 11, 2002, www.cbsnews.com/stories/2002/09/11/60II/main521718.shtml

[9] Meet the Press, September 16, 2001

[10] 60 Minutes II, September 11, 2002, www.cbsnews.com/stories/2002/09/11/60II/main521718.shtml

[11] www.whitehouse.gov

[12] 60 Minutes II, September 11, 2002, www.cbsnews.com/stories/2002/09/11/60II/main521718.shtml

[13] Karen Hughes, Ten Minutes From Normal (New York: Penguin Group, 2004), p236.

[14] www.whitehouse.gov

[15] Bill Sammon, Fighting Back: The War On Terrorism-From Inside the Bush White House (Washington, DC: Regnery Publishing, 2002), p124.

Chapter 8

[1] Ronald Kessler, A Matter of Character: Inside the White House of George W. Bush (New York: Penguin Group, 2004), p130.

[2] 60 Minutes II, September 11, 2002, cbsnews.com/stories/2002/09/11/60II/main521718.shtml

[3]60 Minutes II, September 11, 2002, cbsnews.com/stories/2002/09/11/60II/main521718.shtml

[4]Ari Fleischer, Taking Heat: The President, the Press, and My Years in the White House (New York: William Morrow, 2005), p141.

[5]Bill Sammon, Fighting Back: The War On Terrorism-From Inside the Bush White House (Washington, DC: Regnery Publishing, 2002), p102.

[6]Donald Rumsfeld, DoD News Briefing, September 27, 2001, www.defenselink.mil/transcripts/2001/t09272001_t0927sda.html

[7]Jim Miklaszewski interviews General Myers, msnbc.com/modules/91102/interviews/myers.asp?0cb=-a1a105678&cp1=1

[8]Jim Miklaszewski interviews General Myers, msnbc.com/modules/91102/interviews/myers.asp?0cb=-a1a105678&cp1=1

[9]Ronald Kessler, A Matter of Character: Inside the White House of George W. Bush (New York: Penguin Group, 2004), p142.

[10]Campbell Brown interviews Karl Rove, September 11, 2002, msnbc.com/modules/91102/interviews/rove.asp?0cb=-51a105678&cp1=1

[11]David Gregory interviews Condi Rice, September 11, 2002, msnbc.com/modules/91102/interviews/rice.asp?0cb=-41a105678&cp1=1

[12]60 Minutes II, September 11, 2002, www.cbsnews.com/stories/2002/09/11/60II/main521718.shtml

[13]Meet the Press, September 16, 2001

[14]Meet the Press 9/16/2001

[15]Meet the Press 9/16/2001

[16]Scot J. Paltrow, The Wall Street Journal

[17]Fox News Sunday, September 16, 2001, www.defenselink.mil/transcripts/2001/t09162001_t0916ts.html

[18]9/11 Commission Testimony

[19]Ronald Kessler, A Matter of Character: Inside the White House of George W. Bush (New York: Penguin Group, 2004), p139.

[20]Bill Sammon, Fighting Back: The War On Terrorism-From Inside the Bush White House (Washington, DC: Regnery Publishing, 2002), p102.

[21]By Dan Balz and Bob Woodward, Washington Post, January 27, 2002, www.washingtonpost.com/wp-dyn/articles/A42754-2002Jan26_4.html

Chapter 9

[1]Lisa Myers, MSNBC www.msnbc.com/news/980764.asp?cp1=1

[2]Bill Sammon, Fighting Back: The War On Terrorism-From Inside the Bush White House (Washington, DC: Regnery Publishing, 2002), p103.

[3]Scot J. Paltrow, The Wall Street Journal

[4]Town Hall Meeting, December 4, 2001, www.whitehouse.gov/news/releases/2001/12/20011204-17.html

[5]Scot J. Paltrow, The Wall Street Journal

[6]9/11 Commission Testimony

[7]DoD News Briefing, September 11, 2001, www.defenselink.mil/transcripts/2001/t09112001_t0911sd.html

[8]2004 Republican Convention, www.boston.com/news/politics/conventions/articles/2004/09/01/text_of_dick_cheneys_speech?pg=2

Chapter 10

[1]Bill Sammon, Fighting Back: The War On Terrorism-From Inside the Bush White House (Washington, DC: Regnery Publishing, 2002), p112.

[2]Bill Sammon, Fighting Back: The War On Terrorism-From Inside the Bush White House (Washington, DC: Regnery Publishing, 2002), p112.

[3]Ari Fleischer, Taking Heat: The President, the Press, and My Years in the White House (New York: William Morrow, 2005), p143.

[4]Ari Fleischer, Taking Heat: The President, the Press, and My Years in the White House (New York: William Morrow, 2005), p157.

[5]Bill Sammon, Fighting Back: The War On Terrorism-From Inside the Bush White House (Washington, DC: Regnery Publishing, 2002), p151.

[6]Campbell Brown interviews Karl Rove, September 11, 2002, MSNBC www.msnbc.com/modules/91102/interviews/rove.asp?0cb=-51a105678&cp1=1

[7]Jake Tapper, Salon, http://archive.salon.com/politics/feature/2001/09/11/bush/print.html

[8]Ibid

[9]Bill Sammon, Fighting Back: The War On Terrorism-From Inside the Bush White House (Washington, DC: Regnery Publishing, 2002), p113.

[10]Ari Fleischer, Taking Heat: The President, the Press, and My Years in the White House (New York: William Morrow, 2005), p142.

[11]60 Minutes II, September 11, 2002, www.cbsnews.com/stories/2002/09/11/60II/main521718.shtml

[12]Bill Sammon, Fighting Back: The War On Terrorism-From Inside the Bush White House (Washington, DC: Regnery Publishing, 2002), p108.

[13]Ari Fleischer, Taking Heat: The President, the Press, and My Years in the White House (New York: William Morrow, 2005), p147.

[14]Karen Hughes, Ten Minutes From Normal (New York: Penguin Group, 2004), p243.

[15]Campbell Brown interviews Karl Rove, September 11, 2002, MSNBC www.msnbc.com/modules/91102/interviews/rove.asp?0cb=-51a105678&cp1=1

[16]Karen Hughes, Ten Minutes From Normal (New York: Penguin Group, 2004), p241.

[17]Ibid. p241.

[18]Bill Sammon, Fighting Back: The War On Terrorism-From Inside the Bush White House (Washington, DC: Regnery Publishing, 2002), p113.

[19]60 Minutes II, September 11, 2002, www.cbsnews.com/stories/2002/09/11/60II/main521718.shtml

[20]Bob Woodward, Bush At War (New York: Simon & Schuster, 2002), p 172.

[21]Michael Ventura, Austin Chronicle, www.austinchronicle.com/issues/dispatch/2001-10-05/cols_ventura.html

[22]Bill Sammon, Fighting Back: The War On Terrorism-From Inside the Bush White House (Washington, DC: Regnery Publishing, 2002), p119.

[23]60 Minutes II, September 11, 2002, www.cbsnews.com/stories/2002/09/11/60II/main521718.shtml

[24]60 Minutes II, September 11, 2002, www.cbsnews.com/stories/2002/09/11/60II/main521718.shtml

[25]Carolyn B. Thompson, James W. Ware, The Leadership Genius Of George W. Bush: 10 Commonsense Lessons from the Commander in Chief (New Jersey: John Wiley & Sons, Inc., 2003), p174.

[26]Christopher Andersen, George And Laura: Portrait of an America Marriage (New York: William Morrow, 2002), p5.

[27]Christopher Andersen, George And Laura: Portrait of an America Marriage (New York: William Morrow, 2002), p5.

[28]Karen Hughes, Ten Minutes From Normal (New York: Penguin Group, 2004), p242.

[29]Bill Sammon, Fighting Back: The War On Terrorism-From Inside the Bush White House (Washington, DC: Regnery Publishing, 2002), p128.

[30]60 Minutes II, September 11, 2002, www.cbsnews.com/stories/2002/09/11/60II/main521718.shtml

[31]60 Minutes II, September 11, 2002, www.cbsnews.com/stories/2002/09/11/60II/main521718.shtml

[32]Ari Fleischer, Taking Heat: The President, the Press, and My Years in the White House (New York: William Morrow, 2005), p156.

[33]60 Minutes II, September 11, 2002, www.cbsnews.com/stories/2002/09/11/60II/main521718.shtml

[34]Dennis Prager, March 11, 2003, World Net Daily, wnd.com/news/article.asp?ARTICLE_ID=31468

Chapter 11

[1]Bill Sammon, Fighting Back: The War On Terrorism-From Inside the Bush White House (Washington, DC: Regnery Publishing, 2002), p126.

[2]60 Minutes II, September 11, 2002, www.cbsnews.com/stories/2002/09/11/60II/main521718.shtml

[3]Christopher Andersen, George And Laura: Portrait of an America Marriage (New York: William Morrow, 2002), p13.

Chapter 12

[1]CBS News, March 4, 2004, www.cbsnews.com/stories/2004/03/05/politics/main604202.shtml

[2]Karen Hughes, Ten Minutes From Normal (New York: Penguin Group, 2004), p132.

[3]Karen Hughes, Ten Minutes From Normal (New York: Penguin Group, 2004), p257.

[4]Meet the Press, April 4, 2004, www.msnbc.msn.com/id/4663767/

[5]2004 Republican Convention,
www.washingtonpost.com/wp-dyn/articles/A47237-2004Aug30.html

[6]Vice President's Remarks at a Welcome Rally at Ellis Island, August 29, 2004, www.whitehouse.gov/news/releases/2004/08/20040829-1.html

[7]2004 2nd Debate

[8]Bill Sammon, Fighting Back: The War On Terrorism-From Inside the Bush White House (Washington, DC: Regnery Publishing, 2002), p190.

[9]Bill Sammon, Fighting Back: The War On Terrorism-From Inside the Bush White House (Washington, DC: Regnery Publishing, 2002), p198.

[10]2004 Republican Convention, www.boston.com/news/politics/conventions/articles/2004/08/31/text_of_the_honorable_marc_racicot/

[11]Karen Hughes, Ten Minutes From Normal (New York: Penguin Group, 2004), p253.

[12]2004 Republican Convention, www.boston.com/news/politics/conventions/articles/2004/08/31/text_of_former_nyc_mayor_rudolph_giulianis_speech_before_the_republican_national_convention/

[13]2004 Republican Convention, www.boston.com/news/politics/conventions/articles/2004/09/01/text_of_dick_cheneys_speech/

[14]Karen Hughes, Ten Minutes From Normal (New York: Penguin Group, 2004), p253.

[15]President's Remarks in Cincinnati, Ohio, October 31, 2004, www.whitehouse.gov/news/releases/2004/10/print/20041031-9.html

[16]David Gregory interviews Karen Hughes, September 11, 2002, MSNBC www.msnbc.com/modules/91102/interviews/hughes.asp?0cb=-21a105678&cp1=1

[17]Remarks by the President In Telephone Conversation with New York Mayor Giuliani and New York Governor Pataki, September 13, 2001, www.whitehouse.gov/news/releases/2001/09/20010913-4.html

[18]9/11 Commission Testimony

[19]Rumsfeld Address to the Troops and All Department of Defense Personnel, September 12, 2001, www.defenselink.mil/specials/secdefaddress/

Chapter 13

[1]www.whitehouse.gov

[2]9/11 Commission Testimony

[3]President Holds Prime Time News Conference, October 11, 2001, www.whitehouse.gov/news/releases/2001/10/20011011-7-index.html

[4]9/11 Commission Testimony

[5]Campbell Brown interviews Karl Rove, September 11, 2002, MSNBC www.msnbc.com/modules/91102/interviews/rove.asp?0cb=-51a105678&cp1=1

[6]Lee Troxler (Editor), Fahrenhype 9/11 Companion Book: Unraveling The Truth About Fahrenheit 9/11& Michael Moore (Michael and Me L.P., 2004), p56.

[7]Campbell Brown interviews Karl Rove, September 11, 2002, MSNBC www.msnbc.com/modules/91102/interviews/rove.asp?0cb=-51a105678&cp1=1

[8]David Gregory interviews Karen Hughes, September 11, 2002, MSNBC www.msnbc.com/modules/91102/interviews/hughes.asp?0cb=-21a105678&cp1=1

[9]President's Address to the Nation, November 8, 2001, www.whitehouse.gov/news/releases/2001/11/print/20011108-13.html

[10]John Podhoretz, Bush Country: How Dubya Became A Great President While Driving Liberals Insane (New York: St. Martin's Press 2004), p183.

[11]Lee Troxler (Editor), Fahrenhype 9/11 Companion Book: Unraveling The Truth About Fahrenheit 9/11& Michael Moore (Michael and Me L.P., 2004), p78.

[12]President's Address to the Nation, November 8, 2001, www.whitehouse.gov/news/releases/2001/11/print/20011108-13.html

[13]U.S. Joint Inquiry Staff

[14]President's Address to the Nation, November 8, 2001, www.whitehouse.gov/news/releases/2001/11/print/20011108-13.html

[15]Secretary Rumsfeld Interview with Fox News Sunday, September 16, 2001, www.defenselink.mil/transcripts/2001/t09162001_t0916ts.html

[16]President's Address to the Nation, November 8, 2001, www.whitehouse.gov/news/releases/2001/11/print/20011108-13.html

[17]Statement by DCI Tenet before the Senate Select Committee on Intelligence (SSCI) on the "Worldwide Threat 2001: National Security in a Changing World" (7 February 2001), www.cia.gov/terrorism/pub_statements_terrorism.html

[18]Bill Sammon, Misunderestimated, The President Battles Terrorism, John Kerry, and the Bush Haters (New York: HarperCollins, 2004), p5.

[19]Press Briefing By Ari Fleischer, September 15, 2001, www.whitehouse.gov/news/releases/2001/09/20010915-5.html

[20]Donald Rumsfeld, DoD News Briefing, September 27, 2001, www.defenselink.mil/transcripts/2001/t09272001_t0927sda.html

[21]President Holds Prime Time News Conference, October 11, 2001, www.whitehouse.gov/news/releases/2001/10/20011011-7-index.html

[22]U.S. Joint Inquiry Staff

[23]9/11 Commission Testimony

[24]Karen Hughes, Ten Minutes From Normal (New York: Penguin Group, 2004), p11.

[25]9/11 Commission Testimony

[26]Press Briefing by Ari Fleischer, September 12, 2001, www.allamericanpatriots.com/m-news+article+storyid-1601.html

[27]Press Briefing By Ari Fleischer, September 13, 2001, www.whitehouse.gov/news/releases/2001/09/20010913-12.html

[28]www.whitehouse.gov/infocus/nationalsecurity/faq-what.html

[29]9/11 Commission Testimony

[30]President's Remarks at Victory 2004 Rally in West Chester, Ohio, September 27, 2004, www.whitehouse.gov/news/releases/2004/09/20040927-8.html

[31]Washington Post, September 13, 2001, www.washingtonpost.com/wp-srv/nation/transcripts/bushtext2_091301.html

[32]David Frum, The Right Man (New York: Random House, 2003), p114.

[33]Washington Post, September 12, 2001,www.washingtonpost.com/wp-srv/nation/transcripts/rumsfeldtext_091201.html

[34]2nd Presidential Debate 2004

[35]John Diamond and Kathy Kiely, USA TODAY, May 17, 2002, www.usatoday.com/news/washington/2002/05/17/failure-usatcov.htm#more

[36]Daniel McKivergan, Weekly Standard, www.weeklystandard.com/Content/Public/Articles/000/000/004/737qrycx.asp

[37]1st Presidential Debate 2004

[38]2nd Presidential Debate 2004

[39]John Diamond and Kathy Kiely, USA TODAY, May 17, 2002, www.usatoday.com/news/washington/2002/05/17/failure-usatcov.htm

[40]2004 Republican Convention, www.boston.com/news/politics/conventions/articles/2004/08/31/text_of_sen_john_mccains_speech_before_the_republican_national_convention/

[41]U.S. Joint Inquiry Staff

[42]2004 Republican Convention, www.boston.com/news/politics/conventions/articles/2004/08/31/text_of_sen_john_mccains_speech_before_the_republican_national_convention/

[43]2004 Republican Convention, www.boston.com/news/politics/conventions/articles/2004/09/03/text_of_convention_remarks_by_gen_tommy_franks/

[44]President George W. Bush From his acceptance speech at the Republican National Convention September 2, 2004

[45]President Discusses War on Terrorism, November 8, 2001, www.whitehouse.gov/news/releases/2001/11/print/20011108-13.html

Chapter 14

[1]William Kristol , Weekly Standard, www.weeklystandard.com/Content/Public/Articles/000/000/004/813stdef.asp

[2]George W. Bush, A Charge To Keep (New York: William Morrow & Company, Inc., 1999), p119.

[3]President's Remarks at Victory 2004 Rally in West Chester, Ohio, September 27, www.whitehouse.gov/news/releases/2004/09/20040927-8.html

[4]Lee Troxler (Editor), Fahrenhype 9/11 Companion Book: Unraveling The Truth About Fahrenheit 9/11& Michael Moore (Michael and Me L.P., 2004), p87.

[5]Town Hall Meeting, December 4, 2001, www.whitehouse.gov/news/releases/2001/12/20011204-17.html

[6]Time Magazine, December 31, 1999

[7]www.whitehouse.gov/news/releases/2002/09/20020927-6.html

[8]President Bush Meets with Prime Minister Blair, January 31, 2003, www.whitehouse.gov/news/releases/2003/01/20030131-23.html

[9]Remarks by the President at the 2003 "Congress of Tomorrow" Republican Retreat Reception, February 9, 2003, www.whitehouse.gov/news/releases/2003/02/20030209-1.html

[10]Remarks by the President at the 2003 "Congress of Tomorrow" Republican Retreat Reception, February 9, 2003, www.whitehouse.gov/news/releases/2003/02/20030209-1.html

[11]Richard A. Clarke, Against All Enemies, Inside America's War on Terror (New York: Free Press, 2004), p 110.

[12]The President's State of the Union Address, January 29, 2002, www.whitehouse.gov/news/releases/2002/01/20020129-11.html

[13]www.whitehouse.gov/news/releases/2002/09/20020927-6.html

[14]Sean Hannity, Let Freedom Ring: Winning The War of Liberty Over Liberalism (New York: ReganBooks, 2002) p12.

[15]Meet the Press, September 16, 2001

[16]Meet the Press, April 4, 2004, www.msnbc.msn.com/id/4663767/

[17]www.msnbc.msn.com/id/4694779/

[18]John Diamond and Kathy Kiely, USA TODAY, May 17, 2002, www.usatoday.com/news/washington/2002/05/17/failure-usatcov.htm

[19]David Gregory interviews Condi Rice, September 11, 2002, www.msnbc.com/modules/91102/interviews/rice.asp?0cb=-41a105678&cp1=1

[20]Washington Post, September 13, 2001, www.washingtonpost.com/wp-srv/nation/transcripts/bushtext2_091301.html

[21]Wikipedia.com

[22]Day One Transcript: 9/11 Commission Hearing, March 23, 2004, www.washingtonpost.com/wp-dyn/articles/A17798-2004Mar23.html

[23]9/11 Commission Testimony, www.msnbc.msn.com/id/4693224

[24]9/11 Commission Testimony, www.msnbc.msn.com/id/4693224

[25]9/11 Commission Testimony, www.msnbc.msn.com/id/4693224/

[26]60 Minutes, March 28, 2004, www.cbsnews.com/stories/2004/03/28/60minutes/printable609074.shtml

[27]Full transcript of Rice's 9/11 testimony, www.msnbc.msn.com/id/4694779/

[28]Congressional Record: March 25, 2004

[29]Lee Troxler (Editor), Fahrenhype 9/11 Companion Book: Unraveling The Truth About Fahrenheit 9/11& Michael Moore (Michael and Me L.P., 2004), p56.

Chapter 15

[1]Joseph Curl, Washington Times, October 7, 2004, washtimes.com/national/20041007-014036-2892r.htm

[2]Rudolph W. Giuliani, Leadership (New York: Miramax Books, 2002),

[3]John Diamond and Kathy Kiely, USA TODAY, May 17, 2002, www.usatoday.com/news/washington/2002/05/17/failure-usatcov.htm

[4]Chicago Tribune, November 18, 2001

[5]Secretary Rumsfeld Interview for ABC News This Week, September 16, 2001, www.defenselink.mil/transcripts/2001/t09162001_t0916sd.html

[6]Chicago Tribune, November 18, 2001

[7]Press Briefing by National Security Advisor Dr. Condoleezza Rice, May 16, 2002, www.whitehouse.gov/news/releases/2002/05/20020516-13.html

[8]Los Angeles Times September 27, 2001

[9]Full transcript of Dr. Rice's 9/11 testimony, www.msnbc.msn.com/id/4694779/

[10]9/11 Commission Testimony

[11]Richard A. Clarke, Against All Enemies: Inside America's War On Terror (New York: Free Press, 2004), p108.

[12]MSNBC, April 7, 2004, www.msnbc.msn.com/id/4669499/

[13]Secretary Rumsfeld Interview with Fox News Sunday, September 16, 2001, www.defenselink.mil/transcripts/2001/t09162001_t0916ts.html

[14]Remarks by the President at Presentation of Commander-In-Chief's Trophy, May 17, 2002, www.whitehouse.gov/news/releases/2002/05/print/20020517-1.html

[15]Los Angeles Times September 27, 2001 Thursday

[16]Press Briefing by National Security Advisor Dr. Condoleezza Rice, May 16, 2002, www.whitehouse.gov/news/releases/2002/05/print/20020516-13.html

[17]Press Briefing by National Security Advisor Dr. Condoleezza Rice, May 16, 2002, www.whitehouse.gov/news/releases/2002/05/print/20020516-13.html

[18]Los Angeles Times September 27, 2001

[19]News Conference, October 11, 2001, www.whitehouse.gov/news/releases/2001/10/20011011-7-index.html

[20]Sydney Morning Herald, 9/20/01

[21]Remarks by the President at Presentation of Commander-In-Chief's Trophy, May 17, 2002, www.whitehouse.gov/news/releases/2002/05/20020517-1.html

[22]Press Briefing by National Security Advisor Dr. Condoleezza Rice, May 16, 2002, www.whitehouse.gov/news/releases/2002/05/20020516-13.html

[23]Bob Woodward, Bush At War (New York: Simon & Schuster, 2002), p145.

Chapter 16

[1]Meet the Press, April 4, 2004, www.msnbc.msn.com/id/4663767/

[2]Secretary Rumsfeld Interview with Fox News Sunday, September 16, 2001, www.defenselink.mil/transcripts/2001/t09162001_t0916ts.html

[3]Full transcript of Dr. Rice's 9/11 testimony, www.msnbc.msn.com/id/4694779/

[4]www.cbsnews.com/stories/2004/03/28/60minutes/main609074.shtml

[5]Rita Cosby, Fox News, December 28, 1999

[6]Press Briefing by National Security Advisor Dr. Condoleezza Rice, May 16, 2002, www.whitehouse.gov/news/releases/2002/05/20020516-13.html

[7]Remarks by the President In Telephone Conversation with New York Mayor Giuliani and New York Governor Pataki, September 13, 2001, www.whitehouse.gov/news/releases/2001/09/20010913-4.html

[8]Press Briefing by National Security Advisor Dr. Condoleezza Rice, May 16, 2002, www.whitehouse.gov/news/releases/2002/05/20020516-13.html

[9]Reuters News, April 14, 2004, www.publicbroadcasting.net/vpr/news.newsmain?action=article& ARTICLE_ID=627106

[10]9/11 Commission Testimony, www.msnbc.msn.com/id/4693224/

[11]Press Briefing by Ari Fleischer, September 12, 2001, www.whitehouse.gov/news/releases/2001/09/20010912-8.html

[12]Press Briefing by National Security Advisor Dr. Condoleezza Rice, May 16, 2002, www.whitehouse.gov/news/releases/2002/05/20020516-13.html

[13]Full transcript of Dr. Rice's 9/11 testimony, www.msnbc.msn.com/id/4694779/

Chapter 17

[1]Town Hall Meeting, December 4, 2001, www.whitehouse.gov/news/releases/2001/12/20011204-17.html

[2]David Gregory interviews Condi Rice, September 11, 2002, www.msnbc.com/modules/91102/interviews/rice.asp?0cb=-41a105678&cp1=1

[3]9/11 Commission Testimony, www.msnbc.msn.com/id/4693224/

[4]9/11 Commission Testimony, www.msnbc.msn.com/id/4693224/

[5]Press Briefing by National Security Advisor Dr. Condoleezza Rice, May 16, 2002, www.whitehouse.gov/news/releases/2002/05/20020516-13.html

[6]Press Briefing by National Security Advisor Dr. Condoleezza Rice, May 16, 2002, www.whitehouse.gov/news/releases/2002/05/20020516-13.html

[7]www.whitehouse.gov/news/releases/2002/05/print/20020516-13.html

[8]Full transcript of Dr. Rice's 9/11 testimony, www.msnbc.msn.com/id/4694779/

[9]www.cbsnews.com/stories/2004/03/19/60minutes/main607356.shtml

[10]Press Briefing by National Security Advisor Dr. Condoleezza Rice, May 16, 2002, www.whitehouse.gov/news/releases/2002/05/20020516-13.html

[11]Full transcript of Dr. Rice's 9/11 testimony, www.msnbc.msn.com/id/4694779/

[12]9/11 Commission Testimony, www.theleftcoaster.com/archives/001490.php

[13]9/11 Commission Testimony, www.msnbc.msn.com/id/4693224/

[14]Press Briefing by National Security Advisor Dr. Condoleezza Rice, May 16, 2002, www.whitehouse.gov/news/releases/2002/05/20020516-13.html

[15]Press Briefing by National Security Advisor Dr. Condoleezza Rice, May 16, 2002, www.whitehouse.gov/news/releases/2002/05/20020516-13.html

Chapter 18

[1]Full transcript of Dr. Rice's 9/11 testimony, www.msnbc.msn.com/id/4694779/

[2]Rita Cosby, Fox News, December 28, 1999

[3]9/11 Commission Testimony, www.msnbc.msn.com/id/4693224/

[4]Bob Woodward, Bush At War (New York: Simon & Schuster, 2002), p145.